GEORGIAN JEWELLERY

1714-1830

GEORGIAN JEWELLERY

1714-1830

by Ginny Redington Dawes
with Olivia Collings

Photographs by Tom Dawes

ACC ART BOOKS

First published in 2007 by the Antique Collectors' Club
Reprinted 2010

Published in 2018 by ACC Art Books
Reprinted 2019, 2023

ISBN 978-1-85149-921-2

British Library Cataloguing-in-Publication Data
A catalogue record for this book is available from the British Library

FSC www.fsc.org MIX Paper from responsible sources FSC® C124385

Printed in China
for ACC Art Books Ltd., Woodbridge, Suffolk, UK
www.accartbooks.com

ACC ART BOOKS

The authors in times gone by. A fascination with the eighteenth century seems to have come early to both Ginny Dawes and Olivia Collings. Although they came respectively from the sidewalks of Brooklyn, New York, and the orchards of Kent, England, they were both passionate about jewellery from an early age. Olivia purchased her first piece when she was just seven years old. Ginny was so attached to a little box of broken beads given her by her mother that the surgeon had to pry it from her hands before performing her tonsillectomy at the age of three. Both Ginny's and Olivia's enthusiasm for seeking and studying antique jewels has continued ever since. Ginny's twenty-odd years of writing about and collecting antique jewellery in New York and Olivia's reputation as one of London's most knowledgeable dealers in eighteenth century jewels is the winning equation that has produced *Georgian Jewellery 1714-1830.*

In loving memory of Joan Maxwell

Acknowledgements

Our heartfelt gratitude to our husbands, Tom Dawes and Garth Collings, for their unstinting interest, encouragement and assistance -– we could not have produced this book without Tom's outstanding photography – and to our special friends: Linda Morgan, Charlotte Sayers, Gaby Ruthven and Pat Novissimo, who supported us with their enthusiasm and knowledge. Nor could this book have been realised without the kindness and expertise of the many dealers and collectors on both sides of the Atlantic who loaned us their treasures: Jonathan Norton, Jean Louis Chameroy, Marcie Imberman and Ellen Israel, Olivia Gerrish and Joanna Elton, Lynn and Brian Holmes, Jacky Jacoby, Emily Satloff, Patricia Taub, Peter Hesse, Hannelore Hetteling, Gray Boone, Julie Seitzman, Michele Rowan, Lynn Lindsay, Melody Rodgers, David Lavender, Horatia Sterne, Sian Harlowe, Edith Horowitz, Ian Stanley, Corinne Davidov, Jim Davies, Richard Harrison and Paulette Bates, Leah Gordon, John Joseph, Michael Longmore, Ronald Kawitzky, Donald Edge, Anthea, Jeffrey Shockett, Olga L'Agbesi, Tony Douch, Jackie Smelkinson and Marcia Moylan, Stephen Reynolds, Barbara Shair and Frederica Jaret. Special thanks to our experts in their fields: antiquarian bookseller extraordinaire Henry Polissack, master craftsmen Raymond Shaw and David Quinn, knowledgeable gemmologist Chris Cavey, miniature 'giant' Elle Shushan, financial wizard Susan Ross, and antiquities specialist Peter Szuhay. Our gratitude goes out to Judy Collinson and the team at Barneys New York for their enthusiasm for Georgian jewellery which helped create 'the buzz' that demanded a book such as this. Last but not least, many thanks to Diana Steel and the hard working staff of ACC, and especially to our editor Primrose Elliott, for believing in this project and making it happen so beautifully.

Contents

Preface

For the student and collector of antique jewellery in the twenty-first century, the adjective 'Georgian' has come to be the definitive term and catch-all name for jewellery created between 1714 and 1830 in England and in Europe, during the reigns of the British Kings George I, II, III and IV. Because eighteenth century jewellery was so international in scope, it is often impossible to say with certainty whether a piece is English or Continental in origin unless it exhibits some decidedly regional characteristic. While the prevailing wisdom is that England was the leader in the making of jewellery, the rest of Europe was not far behind. Throughout the next 116 years, jewellery makers of many countries would exchange ideas, follow trends and improve upon one another's designs.

As styles and fashions evolved, jewellery, previously the sole prerogative of the aristocracy, became available to an ever-expanding middle class. Perhaps this explains the significant number of remarkable pieces (from ones that are almost priceless to those that cost very little) which have survived and are still available to view, study and own. It is surprising that to date there has been no book completely devoted to the era that produced some of the most magnificent jewellery ever made. This is what we hope to remedy with *Georgian Jewellery,* a book dedicated to exploring the unparalleled workmanship and beauty of this age and revealing it to the jewellery lovers of today.

Shell cameo of Cupid c.1815

Louis XV French three-colour gold watch with rose cut diamonds, Paris 1767

Boxed flat-cut garnet demi-parure c.1820

This undertaking was not without its challenges. The subject of jewellery was not a priority in the chronicling of Georgian times. There is little knowledge found in contemporary texts and surprisingly scant information to be gleaned from studying paintings. The prevailing style of portraiture throughout most of the Georgian period was for women to be pictured elaborately dressed but unadorned by jewels: glorious wedding-cake hooped gowns of pastel silks and taffetas, hairdos that required more construction than an English castle and yet, strangely, bare ears, necks and wrists! A jewellery trend could last as long as seventy-five years and die out in one location only to pop up in another, making it difficult to be absolutely sure not only where a piece was made, but when. As there is no sole authority on Georgian jewellery, it was necessary to piece together our knowledge from numerous sources to try to fill in the blanks. Fortunately, we discovered rich material in the diaries of Georgian women, ladies' magazines of the day, books of jewellery designs, ledgers of gem-dealers, and the rare portraits of eighteenth century women who actually happened to be wearing jewellery. But, best of all, we found a fantastic body of work by a veritable legion of talented jewellers.

Much fine jewellery was broken up and reset in later periods, but our five year search uncovered many amazing examples of eighteenth century splendour in original unaltered condition. Although most of the jewellery pictured in this book is of English origin, we have included many treasures that are truly international: precious and paste bijoux from France, iron jewellery from Germany, micro-mosaics from Italy, agates from Scotland, topaz and chrysoberyl jewellery from Portugal, and emeralds from Spain. We have taken special interest in pieces exhibiting the unique techniques of the era: cannetille gold work, micro-mosaics, hair work and iron work and the new secondary materials of the age such as pinchbeck, Wedgwood, paste and cut-steel. And, finding resonance in both ends of the spectrum, we have delighted equally in things anachronistic (such as the chatelaine) and the timeless (the diamond ring).

We believe *Georgian Jewellery* will fill a gap in the jewellery collector's library, and, to that end, we have included practical advice on how to recognise it, acquire it, decipher its secrets, wear it and take care of it. But, most of all, we have intended *Georgian Jewellery* to be a feast for the imagination: a stroll back through history to a morning when sunlight streamed down upon a Georgian brick manor house within whose walls characters straight out of Jane Austen were fastening cameos to their necklines and tucking watches on long gold chains into their waistbands; to a gala evening where sumptuous jewels and gemstones glittered and gleamed their way through the candlelight of a palace ballroom; to a time when emotions were expressed by displaying wearable tokens of love, or of sadness, or of mystery – each piece a surviving testimony to another thrilling journey of the human heart.

Opposite:
Garnet, pearl and gold cannetille padlock pendant, 2in. long, c.1820

Below:
Gold textured chain c.1820

Chapter 1
Dawn

'Out of the darkness and into the light!' is an apt way to describe the emerging fashions and jewels of the Georgian period. Into the light of better candles, the better to show off fabulous real and faux gems of amazing clarity and colour. Into the light of less heavy, paler fabrics, thus shedding the dark velvets and brocades of the preceding centuries. Into the light of a profusion of newly discovered diamonds mined in Brazil and finer methods of cutting them so that they sparkled like never before!

It just as easily might describe the voyage on which we hope to take you: from the darkness of insufficient information about this era, and its jewellery, into the light of fuller understanding and appreciation from the perspectives of culture, fashion and history.

Above:
Rock crystal silver-set Portuguese brooch c.1770

Opposite:
Portrait of Queen Charlotte by Thomas Frye
THE METROPOLITAN MUSEUM OF ART, THE ELISHA WHITTELSEY COLLECTION, THE ELISHA WHITTELSEY FUND, 1969 (69.669.1), IMAGE © THE METROPOLITAN MUSEUM OF ART

Previous page:
'The Fair Nun Unmasked' (oil on canvas) by Henry Morland Robert (1730-1797)
©LEEDS MUSEUMS AND ART GALLERIES (TEMPLE NEWSAM HOUSE) UK/THE BRIDGEMAN ART LIBRARY

Below:
Portraits of the four Kings George on English coins

The reign of Georges I to IV

The Georgian kings were descended from Elizabeth Stuart, the daughter of James I. She married the Elector Palatine Frederick V and their daughter Sophia became the heir of Queen Anne of England, the Queen having outlived all her seventeen children. Sophia died just before Queen Anne and so the throne of England passed in 1714 to her son George, the great grandson of James I.

George I came to the English throne from the province of Hanover, Germany, aged fifty-five years old and unable to speak a word of English. He had very little knowledge about his new kingdom and, although he lived in England, it never became his true home. Until he died, he conversed with his ministers in French.

His son, George II, succeeded him in 1727. George was brought up in England and had been a soldier all his life. He married the intelligent and beautiful Caroline of Anspach. Their son and his heir, Frederick, Prince of Wales, died at the age of forty-four, so that when George II passed away in 1760, he was succeeded by his grandson, who became George III.

George III was the first Hanoverian king to be born and educated in England and was to reign for sixty years. He married Charlotte of Mecklenburg-Strelitz in 1761. A wise and kindly king, he liked to live as simply as possible and delighted in his nickname of 'Farmer George'. Unfortunately, his reputation suffered considerably from the American War of Independence and he was held responsible for the loss of the colonies. Because of extreme ill-health, King George III had to grant the Regency to his son, the Prince of Wales, who served as Prince Regent from 1811 to 1820 and then finally, on the death of the King in 1820, became King George IV.

George IV, as the Prince Regent, in 1795 was married briefly and unhappily to Caroline of Brunswick, a relationship that produced a daughter, Princess

18th century velvet and cut-steel purse and cut-steel and glass pearl necklace and earrings

Charlotte. Although he is said to have been a lazy, vain womanizer, his love of the arts, his extravagant patronage of artists and craftsmen in all genres, and his passion for jewellery has left a fabulous legacy of palaces, paintings, and objets d'art in the British Isles. He died in 1830.

The Georgian period stretched over more than one hundred years and during that time life in Great Britain changed rapidly. Agriculture was revolutionised and, as a result, farmers became wealthy and the less fortunate improved their lot. The sumptuary laws, which in many countries had previously controlled what people wore in order to preserve distinctions in rank, became a thing of the past. The American colonies grew strong enough to declare their independence in 1776. The Industrial Revolution changed the face of the country as machinery using steam was installed in factories and workshops. Transport improved rapidly and a network of canals and roads was built so people and goods could move around much more easily. Thanks to the invention of tarmac, a journey from London to Edinburgh that took two weeks in 1745 took only two days in the 1790s. By the time of the death of George IV, railways were beginning and a new era was about to dawn.

Meanwhile, Society was a world of privilege for those of rank and wealth. Vast fortunes were being made and important social position was no longer due solely to birth – a cultivated, educated manner and a private income went a long way in making up for a less than exalted pedigree.

Ladies had remarkable freedom to travel and visit friends and were expected to be well versed in literature, art, music and politics. No longer solely housekeepers and/or decorative companions, they now took part fully in social discourse. From the fashionable balls in London and the Assemblies at the Pump Rooms in Bath and Tunbridge Wells, to the dances and soirées at beautiful country houses, Society sparkled and shimmered ceaselessly. House parties could last for weeks and entertainments were laid on to involve the whole county.

Foiled amethyst and gold necklace c.1820

The Diamond Diadem, 1820

During the reign of George III England was in a golden age of classical architecture and furniture design of exquisite proportion. The great furniture makers Chippendale, Hepplewhite, Sheraton, the innovative potter Wedgwood, architects Adam and Nash, and garden designers such as Capability Brown – all these men left their mark on Great Britain and their influence reaches through the centuries to the present day.

Clothing evolved from the heavy, structured styles of the early part of the eighteenth century to the flowing lines of the Regency period, an elegant simplicity echoed in the clothing of today. Jewellery followed the same evolution from the heavy, ornate insignia worn solely by royalty and aristocracy to that which was purely decorative and fashion inspired.

Shopping for jewellery was an integral part of Georgian life. Nobility had potential enticements brought to their homes for inspection or had viewings in the private upstairs rooms of jewellery and goldsmith shops. These were located on the well-travelled high streets and were decorated with carved and gilded appointments, glass cabinets, large glass windows. For the less wealthy there were any number of fairs and markets where inexpensive items could be found and these could also be had at circulating libraries which women could visit, without fear of immodest behaviour, and make purchases from a small stock of jewellery and trinkets.

All his life the Prince of Wales (George IV) loved jewels and his appetite appears to have been fed from an early age. At two he appeared at a royal ball with his brother Prince Frederick, 'with new point lace tuckers and cuffs, diamonds round their tuckers and diamond belts and the Prince of Wales had diamond buttons down his petticoat'. As he got older, his passion only increased, and he made extravagant purchases both for himself and others.

Trade card from London Jeweller, Goldsmith's of Foster Lane

One of his favourite suppliers was Rundell, Bridge and Rundell, the Court Jewellers, from whom the Prince Regent bought enormous quantities of jewellery. Diamonds, pearls and gemstones flooded into England smuggled by emigrés fleeing the French Revolution and Mr. Rundell was able to buy them cheaply. Bigger and better suites of jewellery were ordered by the nobility, whose craving for fine jewellery was fuelled by the endless whirl of social events hosted by the Prince. In 1820 Rundell made the circlet for his coronation – a magnificent crown of pearls and brilliant diamonds designed as crosses alternating with sprays of patriotic motifs (the rose, the shamrock and the thistle) symbolising the United Kingdom.

George IV adored parties. Splendid balls and dances were held every night of the Season, as well as masquerades where inventive costumes embroidered with real jewels were paraded – although not always to successful effect. Benjamin Disraeli commented on a well-known society lady thus: '…dressed as Cleopatra in a dress literally embroidered with emeralds and diamonds from top to toe, it looked like armour and she like a rhinoceros'. This passion for masquerades was shared by the French. At one famous masked ball at Versailles, Louis XV came disguised, along with some of his courtiers, as a yew tree topiary (see page 71) and met the lady who later became his mistress, Madame de Pompadour.

Right:
A Victorian tribute to the romance of the Georgian masquerade in an enamel on gold demi-parure

Below:
Portrait of Madame de Pompadour by François Boucher c.1750

French gemstone leaf earrings set à jour c.1800

In 1789 the Revolution dramatically changed the tenor of the times in France from gaiety and creativity to fear and chaos. The crown jewels were stolen by the revolutionaries and later sold to pay war debts. For a while France's production of jewellery declined but by 1799, under the new Consulate, the making of quality jewels resumed.

The new order of the day brought about a marked change in fashion and a period of simplicity in dress: transparent white muslin billowed around ladies of fashion and corsets were abandoned. The more daring even damped down the muslin to cling alluringly to their bodies (although they were tightly encased underneath in a kind of stocking). Jewellery, influenced by French Neo-classicism, became particularly light and refined, with intricately crafted gold work and cameos predominating. The restoration of Louis XVIII to the throne in 1815 brought this aesthetic movement to an end, and rich fabrics and hooped dresses with sparkling jewels returned to fashion.

The enduring allure of gemstones

The eighteenth century's love affair with gemstones had its roots in the thirteenth century when talismanic aspects of jewels were an integral part of life. They were worn to encourage the gods to bestow specific desirable qualities upon the wearer or as protection from undesirable conditions. For example, rubies were said to give one inner peace and happiness; sapphires, heavenly good fortune; emeralds, earthly riches; diamonds, protection against enemies and insanity; and amethysts, protection against intoxication!

By the end of the era gemstones were valued more for their power to beautify than for their so-called magical attributes. A French ladies' magazine of the time reported the dictates of fashion: pearls are for girls, diamonds for dowagers, emeralds and amethysts for fashionable married women, garnets (also called vermeil) are for unmarried women, amber is for working girls, and paste is only for actresses. Luckily, women paid little attention to this proclamation.

Portuguese girandole earrings and pendant/brooch mid-18th century

Diamond supremacy

Early in the eighteenth century enamelling, which had previously been the primary decorative technique in jewellery, was no longer widely popular. The divorce of the art of enamelling from that of gem-setting made the new jewellery look much lighter and more feminine and suited the airy new fashions. From the early 1700s, when Venetian Vincenzo Peruzzi invented the brilliant cut for diamonds, coloured stones became less desirable. Brilliant cut diamonds were heavy and extremely costly so, for most of the eighteenth century, the jewels of choice were still foiled rose cut diamonds in silver close-backed settings. This continued to be true until the last quarter of the century, when coloured gemstones returned to favour and beautiful topaz, emerald, and chrysoberyl jewels reclaimed the spotlight, sharing it with brilliant cut diamonds which had become less expensive and more plentiful.

Fine Berlin iron necklace and earrings made in Horovice, Bohemia c.1830

Meanwhile, throughout Europe, indigenous jewellery was being created. The English were turning out cut-steel and Wedgwood, while the French were fashioning sentimental hair jewellery and sparkling paste. Germans jewellers were casting parures out of iron while Italians were carving cameos out of shell and coral.

Fads and fashions

Fashion throughout the Georgian period was a fickle affair: in 1774 small drop earrings were de rigueur. Three months later the style called for no earrings. In 1801 earrings grew to three inches (7.5cm) and longer but, by 1814, with the return of the Bourbons in France, there was a short fashion for no jewellery at all. Asymmetrical designs were popular until the mid-1700s when fashions dictated a return to symmetrical perfection such as seen in sévigné (formal bow) brooches. The emulation of flowers or feathers were two exceptions, but even these were bound or framed by symmetrical ribbons or bows. For a great deal of the era engraved coloured golds were highly desirable, except for a capricious twenty years between 1740 and 1760 when they were shunned – one can only wonder why.

Fads waxed and waned all over Europe, but rarely at the same time. Around 1790 cannetille (exquisite gold wire-work) came into style in England. In Paris, delayed by the Revolution, it flourished after 1815. Cannetille work continued to be fashionable in England and France well into the 1830s with both countries turning out magnificent parures of amethysts, topazes and aquamarines. Cut-steel was truly English in origin but, long after it ceased being popular at home, it was still being made and appreciated in late nineteenth and twentieth century France.

Pink topaz and chrysoberyl cannetille brooch c.1820

In the eighteenth century fashion cultists took centre stage, such as the 'Macaronis' in 1770 and the 'Incroyables' in 1797. The Macaronis were men of extreme and ridiculous fashion who dressed in tight-fitting, brightly-hued clothes, red high heels, great quantities of jewelled buttons and paste or diamond shoe buckles. They embraced the affectation of the quizzing glass the better to ogle the pretty girls and inspect the assembled company upon making a grand entrance. Les Incroyables were slender youths of the Directoire period in France who assumed a bizarre and contradictory way of dressing: large bicorne hats, walking-sticks, layers and layers of foppish scarves, jackets with huge lapels, and outlandish hairdos that resemble some of the 'punk' styles of the 1980s. Unlike the Macaronis, these men did not appear at all interested in women and it has been suggested that this was a homosexual society that combined paradoxical attitudes of machismo with feminine affectation.

'Macaroni' cartoon, 1773

'Les Incroyables' cartoon, c.1797

The Georgian Era began in 1714, but, from the standpoint of jewellery, it did not reach its apex until the last quarter of the century. Consequently, although this book covers 116 years, most of the glorious things we picture here were made and worn in the last fifty of them. Whatever their age, many pieces are as wearable now as they were then. The stylish length for a necklace may vary from season to season, but fabulous jewellery never goes out of fashion.

Above:
Diminutive pavé set rose diamond ball earrings and pendant, early 19th century

Left:
Maltese cross pendant of exceptional quality – open-backed diamonds set in silver and backed in gold

Opposite:
Portrait of Mary Edwards by Hogarth, 1742

The Emancipation of Mary Edwards

Although Georgian women enjoyed many freedoms and advantages that their predecessors were denied, when it came to conjugal love a woman's alternatives to staying in an unhappy marriage were almost non-existent.

Mary Edwards was an heiress who in 1728 at the age twenty-four had inherited a tremendous fortune from her father, Francis Edwards of Welham. She was reputed to be one of the richest women in England. She was good looking and clever and soon was besieged by would-be suitors – but she chose the wrong man. In 1731, a notorious rake and womanizer, Lord Hamilton, godson of Queen Anne, rushed her into a clandestine marriage and she was trapped. Within months he was squandering her money at the gaming tables and by 1733 her riches were dwindling fast. She had, by then, a baby son and, to protect herself from ruin, Mary took a bold and unprecedented step: she managed to remove all records of her marriage from the registers. She replaced the notice of her son's baptism and described herself as a spinster. In this day and age it is difficult to grasp the enormity of her courage, as henceforth she had to bear the label of harlot and her son, a bastard. Nevertheless, she bravely defied all social conventions and went on to lead a happy and successful life. Two years later, Hogarth painted this portrait: a contented and confident woman in full control of her destiny, wearing an enigmatic smile – and fabulous jewels.

Fantastic fringe necklace of gold set garnets made in Perpignan, France, c.1830

Chapter 2

Day

Above:
Foiled topaz cut-down collet necklace in gold, English c.1780 and open-set multicolour gemstone butterfly brooches c.1820

Opposite:
Portrait of Madame de Senonnes wearing her day-time finery, 1814-16, by Jean-August-Dominique Ingres (1780-1867)
LOCALISATION: NANTES, MUSÉE DES BEAUX-ARTS
(C) PHOTOGRAPH RMN/©GÉRARD BLOT

Unlike the Stuart period which preceded it, the Georgian era exuded a feeling of light-heartedness and freedom. Conventions were no longer so restrictive, enabling the Georgians openly to express their individuality. Much of the leisure time of the upper classes was dedicated to social activities; the pursuit of pleasure and a passion for fashion were two of their most absorbing interests. Georgians embraced the country house life: outdoor amusements during the day and an elegant salon life at night. This new way of living brought about a need for the distinction between day and evening jewellery. For daytime dress Georgian women accessorised their favoured fabrics of broadcloth, doeskin, taffeta, lace, cotton and muslin with compatible materials such as garnets, coral, agate, turquoise, steel and Wedgwood.

Above:
Column of late 18th century closed-back gemstone and diamond gold shanked Georgian rings

Right, above:
Foiled gemstone and natural pearl lace pins, rings and pendant 1785-1820

Right, below:
Collection of poissarde hoop earrings 1790-1810, France, Germany and Italy

A Georgian woman's basic daytime jewellery consisted of a necklace, perhaps of agate or coral, or a gold chain, or chains, sometimes with a watch attached. The brooches of choice were oval cameos worn on the bodice of a dress or lace pins used to fasten a shawl. Rings were often dainty with a central coloured gemstone flanked by a small diamond on each shoulder of the shank. Some ladies would wear a ring on every finger. Bracelets were worn in pairs, either one on each wrist or together, and by the end of the 1820s were being worn a half a dozen at a time. Earrings were usually lightweight. From small single-drop earrings, to rounded hinged hoops, to long dangling pinchbeck torpedoes, every length of earring was

Late 18th century gold and garnet hoop earrings

Unusual foiled rose diamond and silver three-way pendent earrings backed in gold, French c.1780

Two pairs of 18th century torpedo earrings, the left pair in gold, the right in pinchbeck

in style for day wear. Day/night earrings were an attractive and convenient invention consisting of an earring top that could be separated from its drop, so a lady could wear either the top alone or the top and drop together depending on the time of day or the occasion. In France, Germany and Italy, the *poissarde* (French for fishwife) was popular. So called because they were first worn by fishwives selling their wares in Les Halles market in Paris (c.1795), these were hoop earrings with a back-to-front fitting that resembled a fish-hook. They were made of lightweight gold, either plain, stamped or filigreed, and were sometimes embellished with modest gemstones or enamel-work.

Chatelaines, buckles, buttons

The most important article of female daytime jewellery was the chatelaine (the equivalent of today's Swiss Army knife). Attached to it a lady carried her keys, her quizzer, her étui (sewing kit), a note pad and pencil and various other useful items. Some of the earliest eighteenth century chatelaines were quite fragile, made of pierced and chased gold and bedizened with gemstones and enamel work. More frequently, they were much sturdier and made of pinchbeck (an amazing faux gold alloy) or cut-steel. As the century progressed, women hung more and more items from their chatelaines: lockets, watches, scissors, seals, rulers and compasses. This collection of one's indispensable items was known by the French word *equipage.*

The most important item of male daytime dress was the shoe buckle. Throughout the eighteenth century men's shoe buckles were worn by nearly all classes and could be fashioned of almost anything from gold to pinchbeck, diamonds to paste, and cut-steel to silver, according to one's means and status. In the earlier part of the century, gentlemen's clothes were made of velvets, brocades and embroidered silks and the accompanying buttons and buckles were equally costly. Court dress continued to be opulent until the early 1800s, but everyday dress had, by that time, given way to a more austere and aesthetic style consisting of sombre colours, such as dark green and navy blue, browns and blacks, with fine linen and elegant, close-fitting coats. The buckles worn by these gentlemen are now highly collectable and beautiful pairs can still be found, sometimes in their original boxes. Memoirs of the Comtesse de Boigne mention that in 1789, having escaped from France to Brighton at the age of nine, she was brought to the house of Mrs. Fitzherbert and the Prince of Wales who were living as man and wife. She recounts: 'I remember that I was taken one morning to see Mrs. Fitzherbert and that she showed us the Prince's dressing room, where there was a large table entirely covered with shoe buckles. I expressed my astonishment at the sight, and Mrs. Fitzherbert, with a laugh, opened a large cupboard, which was also full; there were enough buckles for every day of the year'.

Mid-18th century cut-steel chatelaine, probably made in Woodstock, England

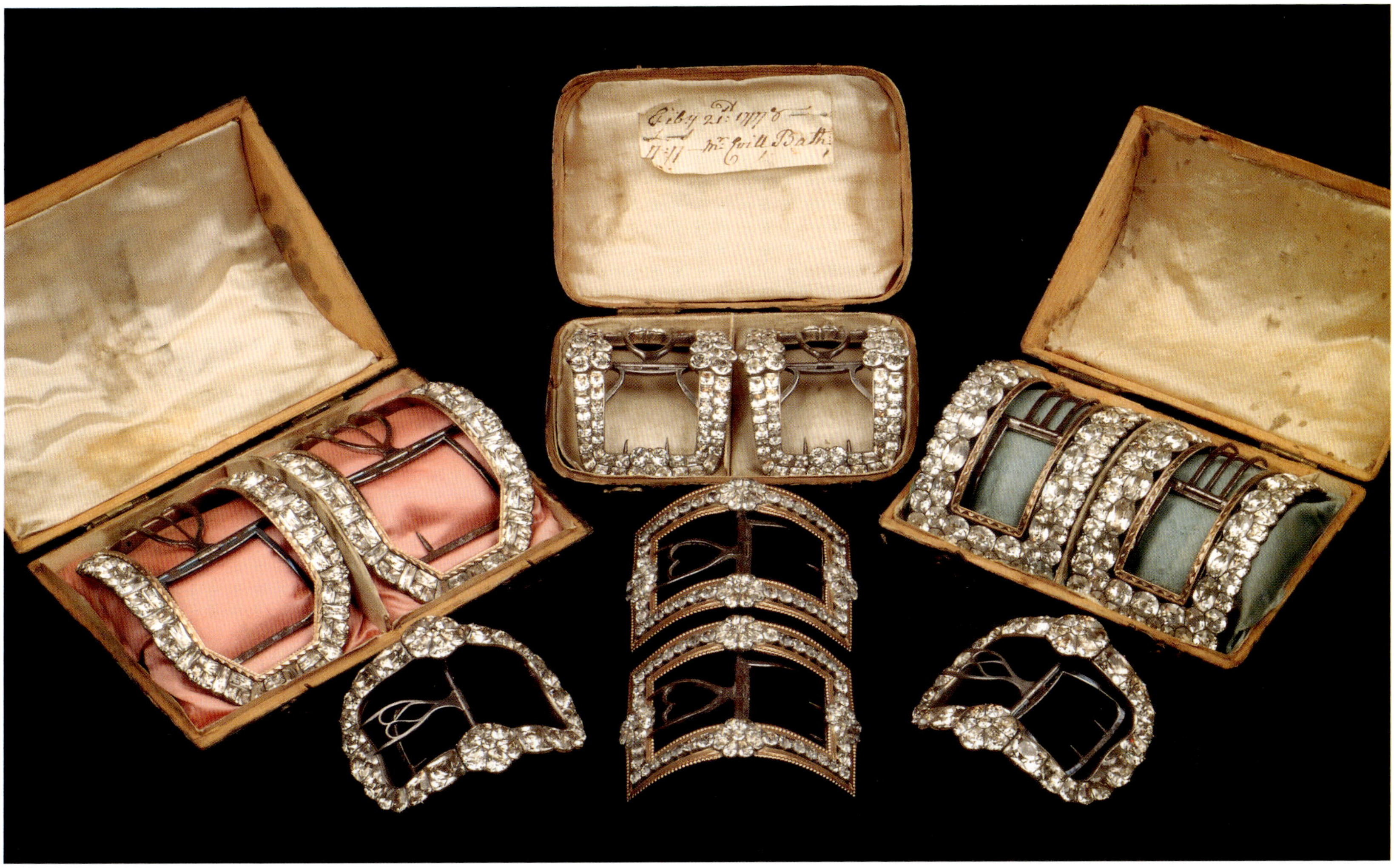

Above:
Men's paste shoe buckles set in silver and gold, late 18th century, boxed

Below:
Paste and silver buttons c.1830

The shoe buckle mania was even illustrated in literature when dramatist Richard Sheridan's Lord Foppington complained to his jeweller: 'My good sir, you forget that these matters are not as they used to be; formerly, indeed, the buckle was a sort of machine, intended to keep on the shoe; but now the case is quite reversed, and the shoe is of no earthly use, but to keep on the buckle!'

Gentlemen's buttons were immensely varied, made from paste, diamonds, gold, silver, steel, ivory and horn.

Above left:
18th century Georgian chains, the outer one of pinchbeck, the inner one of gold

Above right:
Ornate gold 18th century chains

Right:
Long engraved link chains of silver and gold c.1830

Below:
Details of silver belcher chains of varying thickness c.1820

The Georgian chain

There is no item of jewellery more distinctly Georgian than the long gold chain of woven, knitted, engraved or stamped-out links usually joined end to end with a decorative clasp such as an outstretched hand or a barrel studded with tiny gemstones. The more intricate of these might take many weeks to make. The pattern of the links on Georgian chains reveals an endless array of stamped dots, stars, stripes or circles that were impressed on to fine gold sheeting and almost seamlessly joined together. Besides gold, chains were made in a variety of other materials such as iron, steel, gilt metal and pinchbeck. Rarer than these are Georgian chains made of silver. They are almost always worked in the same styles as those made of gold but when seen in silver (especially when they have been allowed to tarnish) are a subtler sort of decoration, antique yet timeless.

Above:
Gold, ebony and ivory cameo esclavage necklace with ribbon-back fittings, French c.1790

Right:
French provincial lightweight gold earrings c.1800

In France the chains of this period tended to be flat, gold links of differing shapes and colours of gold. A favoured style in France in the late 1700s was the *collière d'esclavage* (slave necklace) which combines many of these different links in swags of varying lengths and multiple rows, secured by cameos or plaques at symmetrical points around its circumference. These necklaces are discussed in *The Lady's Magazine* of June 1790: 'The French call them *esclavages* but in this they allude to the natural bondage in which beauty holds mankind, and not the popular idea of enslavement'.

Three pairs of pinchbeck and paste bracelets/ chokers c.1800

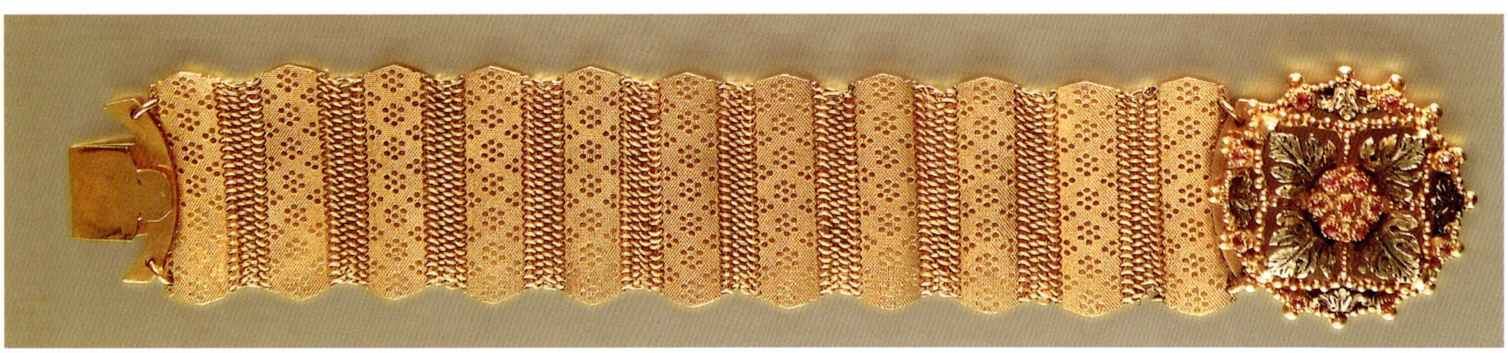

Pinchbeck and red paste en tremblant daisy tiara c.1770

The secret formula of Christopher Pinchbeck

Christopher Pinchbeck (1670–1732) was reputed to be an alchemist – searching for a formula that would turn base metal into gold. Although he didn't achieve this particular goal, he did invent a remarkable metal in 1720 which had all the appearance of fine gold and did not tarnish or deteriorate. This made his fortune as the material became desirable in its own right. Pinchbeck is an alloy of copper and zinc with some secret extra ingredient or method of working it.

Edward Pinchbeck continued the family business after the death of his father and complained bitterly about the inferior gilt metal alloys produced by his rivals to the extent of taking out an advertisement which appeared in the *Daily Post* in London on 11 July 1733:

> Caution to the Publick. To prevent for the future the gross imposition that is daily put upon the Publick by a great number of Shop-Keepers, Hawkers, and Pedlars, in and about this town Notice is hereby given that the Ingenious Mr. Edward Pinchbeck, at the Musical Clock in Fleet Street does not dispose of one grain of his curious metal, which so nearly resembles Gold in Colour, Smell and Ductility, to any person whatsoever nor are the Toys made of the said metal sold by any one person in England except himself....

It carries on in indignant tone – obviously designer fakes are not confined only to the present century!

Pinchbeck was so good a gold substitute that there was a movement by the goldsmiths of the time to prevent it being used for jewellery and, for a brief period, only practical items were manufactured which could not be mistaken for gold. The many and varied items made of the 'real thing' are indeed very beautiful but, unfortunately, the secret of making the original metal is reputed to have died with Edward Pinchbeck and certainly later versions are inferior.

Flat cut garnet and gold demi-parure of naturalistic flower and foliate design c.1820

Garnets

The most desirable gemstone of Georgian day jewellery was undoubtedly the garnet. Jewellers took flat-cut garnets, foiled them (enhancing the stones by placing a tinted metallic foil underneath) to the rich colour of crimson, and arranged them in pleasing naturalistic flower and foliate designs. They were presented in large parures (sets) replete with earrings, pairs of bracelets that formed a choker, hair ornaments, and necklaces possessing a removable pendent drop, some of which have a pin-back mechanism which allowed it also to be worn as a brooch. These drops were often in the shape of a Maltese cross, which was made popular by Lady (Emma) Hamilton, Lord Nelson's mistress, who had collected money and food for the beleaguered Maltese at the end of the eighteenth century when they were being invaded by France. What started out as a wearable medal for good works quickly became a fashionable pendant worn by English women everywhere.

Flat cut garnet jewellery was in demand in the eighteenth century, as it was affordable, attractive on almost every complexion, and looked particularly well on young women. The range of colours depended on whether the garnet was almandine (which, when foiled, was tinged pink, red or purple) or hessonite (tinged orange, red or rust). The pieces from the mid-1700s were chokers, often set in silver. The later pieces (c.1780) were necklets set in gold.

Another style of garnet jewellery which was in vogue during the late eighteenth and early nineteenth centuries was made in Perpignan, France. Local garnets there were faceted like rose-cut diamonds and set as simple

Above:
Gilt metal and flat cut garnet pendeloque earrings c.1750

Left:
Rose-cut garnet and gold rivière necklace and brooch, Perpignan, France c.1830

Almandine garnet earrings set in gold, Perpignan, France, c.1830

rivières (graduated strands of set gemstones) or more elaborate spiky fringed necklaces (such as the one pictured in this chapter heading, page 28). Perpignan is located near the foothills of the Pyrenees and the north-east border of Spain. The garnet industry there dates back to the seventeenth century when the stones were extracted from mines in Estagel, Costabonne and the Col de la Batailleis. Perpignan garnet jewellery was set in gold and foiled to a distinctive deep-pink hue and its unique characteristics reflected the influence of both countries.

While garnet jewellery fell out of favour after 1820, it experienced a revival around 1880. Upon examination, however, it is easy to identify these Victorian pieces as they are lighter in weight, usually set in a lower carat gold, and the work is not as fine as that of the Georgian era.

Above:
Vauxhall glass and metal hairpins, early 19th century

Below:
Cobalt blue Vauxhall glass swag necklace with cross pendant c.1820

Vauxhall glass

Vauxhall glass jewellery was made at the Vauxhall Glassworks in London from the eighteenth century through the mid-nineteenth. It is believed that these trinkets were sold as souvenirs at the nearby Vauxhall Pleasure Gardens (a twelve acre park on the south side of the Thames where Londoners gathered to walk, dine, dance and court). Vauxhall glass necklaces, bracelets, earrings, brooches and hair combs were created in the shapes of butterflies, snowflakes, flowers and crosses on a polished metal backing. They are known for their intense colours (red, blue, green, silver, purple, orange and almost black) and the reflective mirror-like quality of the glass. Although the roots of Vauxhall glass are firmly entrenched in the eighteenth century, many pieces that have been thought to be Georgian are actually Victorian, as enthusiasm for this material lasted for many decades. Victorian pieces, however, are easily recognised as such by their registry marks.

Cross of St. George in Vauxhall glass

Selection of opaline glass jewellery c.1800

Opaline and white paste butterfly clasp c.1790

Opaline glass

Opaline glass, also called opal paste, was made in Derbyshire, England, and in France. This is a faux gem made of glass with a pale, variegated, milky appearance caused by the separation of various oxides during the cooling process of its manufacture. It was usually cut *en cabochon* and tinged pink/blue by setting the paste over rose coloured metallic foil. The English firm of Wickes and Netherton was one of the companies known for its production and advertised it as 'false-work'. Although it bears little resemblance to the gemstone for which it was named, opaline glass was favoured for daytime fashion and was particularly attractive when combined with white paste.

Carved ivory floral brooch c.1825

Italian cameo pendant of amber, first quarter of 19th century, set in an 18th century frame of emeralds, rubies and diamonds

Materials found in nature

Existing alongside the desire for the richly saturated colours of paste and glass faux jewels was the eighteenth century woman's appreciation for things natural. Aesthetic taste had become highly refined and materials such as agates, coral, turquoise, cornelian, pearls, ivory and amber were highly prized for their natural beauty. Round or barrel-shaped, smooth or faceted, beaded strands of

Above:
Pavé set turquoise snake buckle with diamond head and similar ring c.1820

Opposite:
Amber, coral and turquoise beads c.1830

Above:
Yew tree wood and gold rivière necklace, 1820

Right:
Detail of inscription on back of yew wood rivière

amber, turquoise and coral were the perfect necklaces for daytime. Carved into delicate floral sprays or branches, ivory brooches and earrings were attractive accessories. Parures of coral cameos from Italy were mounted simply and smartly. Even wood could make an effective jewellery material, as evidenced by the wooden rivière made of Queen Mary's yew from Crookston Castle, Glasgow.

Italian natural pearl and gold ribbon tie necklace with earrings c.1780

A pool of Oriental pearls with rose diamond clasps

Pearls

The ancients thought that pearls were formed by oysters opening up to heaven and catching drops of dew which then became pearls, but finally it was noticed that no one had actually caught oysters behaving in this exotic manner and gradually the true cause of the formation of this most magical of gems came to be understood.

Pearls are formed by layer upon layer of nacre building up, around an irritant, to create the iridescent perfection known as the orient of the pearl. Many of the pearls in Georgian jewellery are from the *Pinctada radiata* oyster which was found in the Persian Gulf, the Red Sea and the waters around Sri Lanka.

Above:
Boxed seed pearl necklace with amethyst centred brooch c.1810

Right:
French pearl, ruby and emerald poissarde earrings in original box c.1780

Far right:
Seed pearl and foiled amethyst earrings c.1810

Throughout the ages pearls have been admired and desired and have been exchanged for enormous sums of money. Before Mikimoto developed the cultured pearl in the early 1900s, the lustre and radiance of the natural pearl was widely used in jewellery and decoration. When the cultured pearl was perfected, the value of natural pearls tumbled for a while but now their rarity and beauty command enormous prices. Sadly, marine pollution and the overfishing of the oyster banks has left the natural pearl in extreme jeopardy and the population of the *Pinctada radiata* oyster, which yielded the fabled Oriental pearls, in serious decline.

Coque de perle graduated necklet set in gold c.1780

Seed pearls, tiny natural pearls from India, were an essential part of Georgian jewellery. They were made into long tasselled sautoirs, or threaded into intricate designs to support slides and clasps, or used as surrounds for gemstones. Particularly exquisite are the parures of seed pearls in various sizes, sewn by hand on to a drilled mother-of-pearl backing to create necklaces, hair ornaments and earrings of delicate beauty. Occasionally these are set with gemstone-mounted centres. For all its fragility, a good deal of seed pearl work has survived and fine examples in boxed sets can still be found.

Pearls have always had a beautifying effect on women. Lady Sarah Bunbury declared in 1762: 'My hoggy paws are pretty – very much improved by the pearl bracelets'. These were probably multi-strands of pearls worn in pairs. The most important decorative part of a bracelet was its clasp and this was often set with a miniature or cameo surrounded by – what else? – pearls!

Faux Pearls

As natural pearls always commanded great prices, imitations and substitutes were constantly being invented. Especially lovely are the blown glass 'pearls' that were made with an inner coating of nacre created by making a paste from fish scales which gave these faux gems the appearance of large, natural pearls.

Coque de perle was made from the oval section of the shell of the pearly mollusc, the nautilus, found only in the East Indies. As a jewellery material, it was prized for its lustrous mother-of-pearl iridescence, but had to be weighted with cement to give it body and make it less fragile. It was used to great effect in Georgian jewellery, sometimes set in gold but usually partnered with cut-steel or pyrites.

Blown glass faux pearl earrings with gold fittings c.1780

Right:
Boxed set of coral bead necklace, bracelets and earrings c.1820

Below:
Carved coral jewellery – 'pineapple' carved beads, bracelet, child's bracelet and cornucopia brooch c.1820

Ribbon-tie necklace of backed agates with paste surrounds c.1780

Coral

Coral is a hard, organic substance made of the skeletons of certain undersea polyps. Its colours range from pinkish-white (angel skin) to oxblood red. Attractive and desirable throughout most of the Georgian era, coral had the distinction of being the only natural material that was equally at home for day (called undress), late afternoon (half-dress), or for evening (full dress). For undress, ladies wore coral cameos made in Naples, frequently carved as rosettes, acorns or cherubs' heads; for half-dress, strands of graduated carved beads in faceted or crosshatched ('pineapple') patterns; and for full dress, sets of coral which included necklaces, bracelets and hair combs. In the first few years of the early 1800s it was even combined with diamonds for evening dress. By 1820 it had fallen slightly from favour, to be confined once again to half-dress.

Agate

The finest Georgian agate jewellery had faceted or cabochon stones cut in fine, translucent slivers to allow the light to shine through and reveal the endless variations of the stones. Rivières of graduated and matched stones were often set in gold cut-down settings, and were beautiful and elegant daywear

worn with matching long articulated earrings. Agate is a variety of chalcedony that has variegated bands or stripes of colour and transparency. It often contains inclusions of other minerals which can appear as cloud or tree-like, dendritic formations. Such material is known as moss agate, although the inclusions are not vegetable at all, and the 'moss' can be black, red or brown – or even a combination of all three. Some of these stones can seem to depict a dreamy landscape of trees and fine examples were frequently set into rings. This effect was so popular it was also imitated with embroidered hair, or painted on ivory in sepia tones.

Above:
Three 18th century rings inspired by agate: left, hair with garnet surround; centre, painted ivory flowers with diamond surround; right, embroidered hair to resemble moss agate with diamond surround

Left:
Bracelet of gold and variegated agates in fitted box, Scotland c.1830

Opposite:
Translucent moss agate butterfly brooch with 3½in. long matching earrings set in gold, c.1820

Multicoloured hardstone cameo parure c.1800

Cameos and intaglios

Cameos and intaglios are categorised together because they are both made by carving into hardstones, but in cameos the carved design stands out in relief from its background whereas in intaglios the design is carved into the surface of the gem.

Carvers of hardstone cameos of agate, onyx, malachite or lapis used the natural bands of colour to create a three-dimensional effect which exhibited

great detail and could be polished to a bright shine. These were mostly made in Italy. Travellers doing the Grand Tour of Europe brought home fine examples in both contemporary and classical motifs. Besides mythological deities, cameos often portrayed notable persons, from philosophers to nobility. The Emperor Napoleon I of France chose to decorate his Empress with classical cameos mounted into a diadem, necklaces and bracelets.

Two hardstone cameos: top, Cupid and Psyche c.1800; bottom, Zeus c.1800

Shell cameo swag necklace with scenes of frolicking putti c.1810

Another sort of cameo used extensively at this time was the less costly but still very fine shell cameo, often carved from large natural seashells such as the helmet-shaped *Cassis tubarosa*. Lighter in weight and possessing less detail, most of these were also made in Italy and were used for mythological subjects, such as Cupid and Psyche, and set into parures of jewellery.

Unlike cameos, which are usually large and dramatic, intaglios are smaller and more understated. When they weren't set in gold and used as seals or rings, these were often mounted as necklaces and bracelets in fine settings of gold.

Group of rare blackamoor seals of hardstones embellished with diamonds, mid-18th century

Detail of intaglios of blackamoor seals

Above:
Collection of Tassie seals bearing various mottoes c.1790

Below:
Tassie cameo of George IV as a young Prince set under glass with diamond surround c.1785

Tassies

James Tassie (1735-1799) made well-executed copies of agates and gemstones in moulded glass. He produced over 15,000 cameos and intaglios. Some were of classical subjects, some were portrait medallions of royal or famous people, and some were engraved with proverbs or sentimental sayings in either English or French. He also made models for Josiah Wedgwood (1730-1795) to use for casting his jasperware medallions. Catherine the Great of Russia had an enormous collection of Tassies and valued them for their fine quality and painstaking attention to detail.

Wedgwood

Wedgwood jewellery, a distinctly English phenomenon, was the result of the inspired combination of ceramic-ware plaques made by Josiah Wedgwood & Sons into brooches, pendants, rings, buckles, clasps and earrings with a surround of gold, silver, marcasite, or of cut-steel, frequently made by the great steel jewellery maker, Matthew Boulton of Birmingham (1730-1809). The ceramic is called jasperware and is most often seen in white, light blue, dark blue, lilac, sage green, yellow and black. With its soft, matt finish, it was a perfect material for cameos (which Wedgwood made in great numbers). Perhaps most impressive are the Wedgwood beaded necklaces, delightful confections in pale sherbet colours, adorned with tiny jasperware florets, often finished with cut-steel chain links and embellishments.

Opposite: *Wedgwood and steel jewellery c.1780*

Micro-mosaic and gold swag necklet depicting birds with Roman artefacts c.1810

Opposite:
Two Berlin iron necklaces and earrings with polished steel cameos depicting mythological scenes c.1815

Mosaics and micro-mosaics

Made in Rome and Florence and dating from the early 1800s are some of the loveliest and most unusual pieces of day jewellery: hardstone mosaic plaques that have been set as brooches or earrings in gold or as necklaces and bracelets swagged together with fine gold chain. The subjects are either naturalistic, such as flowers and animals, or architectural, such as Roman antiquities. The finest of these utilise subtly shaded, densely packed, minuscule tesserae and are called micro-mosaics.

Iron and steel

Amid the luxurious precious stone and gold work of the Georgian era, nothing stands out quite as surprisingly as the jewellery made of unusual metals such as iron and steel.

It is believed that the process of making black-lacquered cast iron jewellery, called Berlin iron, originated with the Gleiwitz Foundry in Silesia, Prussia, in the late 1790s, but was taken up shortly thereafter by the Royal Berlin Foundry in Berlin in 1804. Its manufacture flourished simultaneously in Horovice, Bohemia. French production of iron jewellery, it is thought, began two years later, when Napoleon marched on Berlin, confiscated the casting moulds and brought them back to France. Berlin iron did not gain international attention until the Napoleonic Wars (1813-15), however, when Germany asked its wealthy to contribute their precious jewels to the war effort and gave her patrons, in return, iron jewellery that bore the inscription 'Gold gab ich für Eisen 1813' (I gave gold for iron). It is ironic that the very jewellery Napoleon had so valued contributed to his downfall. Berlin iron's popularity did not end with the war. Its unique style had an appeal throughout Europe, and it was often worn as mourning jewellery in France, England, and Germany.

Berlin iron was made by moulding shapes in wax, impressing these shapes in a fine sand and then filling the impressions with molten iron. The cast pieces were left to cool, finished by hand and lacquered black. The most common examples of this jewellery are parures as well as rings, combs, and fans. Many fine examples have been embellished with bright steel accents. It is not unusual to see Berlin iron crosses, as thousands of these were produced to commemorate the death of Queen Luisa of Prussia.

Berlin iron jewellery underwent three distinct transitions in design. The earliest pieces were most often of the neo-classic school: medallions and cameos portraying classical figures linked by decorative chains, sometimes of iron mesh. Around 1815 there was a shift toward realism and designs became leafy, floral and naturalistic. From 1825 on the trend in Berlin iron jewellery was toward Gothic Revival and many of the pieces look like ornate miniature wrought iron gates. Berlin iron continued to be made well into the mid-1800s, but the consensus is that most post-1830 pieces lack the workmanship of the earlier years.

Although most Berlin ironwork is not signed, it becomes more historically significant when it is. The most famous designers who sometimes signed their work were Geiss, Lehmann, Hossauer, and Devaranne. Some Berlin iron is enhanced by gold work, and these pieces are particularly desirable. One of the more important designers of Berlin iron jewellery was Karl Schinkel, who worked for the Berlin foundries and is said to have developed the Gothic Revival style that suits Berlin iron so perfectly.

Pair of Berlin iron earrings, 4in. (10cm) long, c.1830

Opposite:
Far left: *Two pairs of Gothic Revival Berlin iron bracelets which convert into chokers. Pair on left signed Geiss c.1825*

Left: *Naturalistic Berlin iron necklace, Horovice, Bohemia c.1820*

Silesian iron wire-work necklace and bracelet c.1825

Particularly distinctive is the jewellery made of very fine strands of black or grey iron wire mesh and thought to have been produced by the earliest foundry in Silesia. Silesian wire runs the gamut from work that is extremely delicate to pieces that bear an uncanny resemblance to Brillo pads! Wire-work jewellery was also made of steel mesh and produced in Woodstock, England, usually embellished with steel sequins, or paillettes, in the shape of flower heads, stars and butterflies.

Fine Berlin iron bracelet and cross decorated with steel sequins, Gleiwitz c.1815

18th century mesh bracelets with sequin paillettes, similar earrings and a fine Silesian chain with cross

Polished 'sliced' steel chain, watch chain and flat sequin steel earrings c.1780

The superb cut-steel chains such as Matthew Boulton made for Queen Charlotte in 1767 are of lasting appeal and prized today. They were extremely costly, fashioned of thin beautifully polished cut-steel slices in circular and floret shapes. These pieces do not mimic precious jewels but are strong and striking, revealing that steel in its own right can be an arresting ornamentation.

Because cut-steel was primarily a night-time adornment, worn in the flickering glow of candles as a diamond substitute (or perhaps, to some tastes, a diamond improvement!) we have saved the better part of our discourse on cut-steel for our chapter called 'Night'.

Opposite:
Caricature of Beau Brummell by Dighton

Beautiful Beau

George Bryan Brummell (1778-1840), known as Beau Brummell, was England's most famous dandy and *the* arbiter of good taste during its Regency period. He always wore a perfectly tailored dark blue coat, doeskin breeches, top boots and a white muslin cravat which it was rumoured could take him five hours to tie to perfection. He was the epitome of understatement, limiting his jewellery to a diamond cravat pin, his seals and the gold buttons on his superbly tailored cut-away coat. He alone halted the more outlandish excesses in men's dress and made restraint and elegance fashionable.

He has been credited with many sartorial innovations including the precursor of the modern suit and tie which, to this day, are the accepted business and formal attire for gentlemen. He also replaced the top boot with the 'Hessian' boot with its heart-shaped top and tassel. He recommended champagne as the best boot polish.

He was known for his amiability and wit and was a great friend of George IV but unfortunately had a life-changing falling out with him. Upon being cut by King George, he asked a mutual acquaintance within the King's earshot: 'Alvanley, who's your fat friend?' This outrageous remark was to go down in history and undoubtedly contributed to the downward spiral the rest of his life was to be. He fled England after accruing thousands of pounds of debts to tradesmen (most likely his Conduit Street tailor, his St. James's Street bootmaker and his French wine merchants) and died penniless in France.

Highest quality white paste pansy necklace with oversized pendent drop and long rose cut diamond earrings all set in silver and backed in gold, c.1800

Chapter 3

Night

Emerald and diamond oak leaf and acorn tiara c.1830

Richard Rush, the American ambassador to the Court of George IV, described a magnificent ball he attended in 1818 as 'Fairyland… No lady was without her plume. The whole was a waving field of feathers. Some were blue like the sky tinged with red, here you saw violet and yellow, there shades of green. But most were like tufts of snow. The diamonds encircling them caught the light… and threw dazzling beams around… it seemed as if a curtain had risen to show a pageant in another sphere'.

Diamonds

The diamond is among the rarest and most valuable of all precious stones. Carbon in its purest form, it is the hardest and most durable natural substance on earth. Diamonds are graded on four attributes: colour, cut, clarity and carat. Colour should be transparent or near transparent (with the exception of the rare coloured diamonds that are so fashionable today). Over time, the cut of diamonds has evolved from the simple table cut of the sixteenth and seventeenth centuries (flat on top and faceted on its sides), to the rose cut of the eighteenth and nineteenth centuries (whose crown is divided into a series of triangular facets and whose base is flat), to the early brilliant cut – sometimes called an old mine cut – of the mid-eighteenth century (with its many different shaped and sized facets over a very small culet allowing the least amount of light to escape through the bottom of the stone). This was the

Opposite:
Engraving by Charles-Nicolas Cochin of the The Yew Tree Ball (Le Bal des Ifs) in 1745 where Madame de Pompadour first met her future paramour, King Louis XV, who came to the masquerade with his courtiers all dressed as yew tree topiaries
The Metropolitan Museum of Art
Harris Brisbane Dick Fund, 1930 (30.22(34.34)
Image ©The Metropolitan Museum of Art

Foiled rose cut diamond bow-drop earrings closed-set in silver c.1780

forerunner of the modern-day brilliant cut whose supremacy in showing off a diamond to its best effect has never been surpassed. Clarity of stones is judged by the absence, or triviality, of flaws, and, of course, a larger carat weight, in combination with the above three factors, is the determinant in assessing the value of a particular diamond.

When considering diamonds in antique jewellery, however, there are many other factors to evaluate, the most important of which is the actual beauty of the stone in its original antique setting. It might even be said that early diamonds have an allure and mystery that are sometimes more entrancing for their imperfect shapes.

Left:
Three diamond bracelets, c.1780-1820. The one at the far left features the symbol of the Order of the Golden Fleece, which was awarded by the Hapsburgs to European nobility

Opposite:
Closed-back old cut diamond flower and foliate necklace set in silver and gold c.1800

Foiled smoky quartz rivière with detachable Maltese cross and drop earrings c.1810

The rivière

The most timeless Georgian night-time necklace was the diamond rivière – literally a river of light – as simple and beautiful now as it was then. Tradition has it that the Riviera in the South of France was so called because from out at sea, on your yacht, the sparkling lights of the Côte d'Azur looked like a glittering necklace. Rivières were made of graduated collet-set matched stones connected together as unobtrusively as possible. Silver-set diamond rivières achieved popularity around 1750 but, by 1767, as a result of an innovation achieved by the jeweller, James Cox, they were mounted in silver but backed with gold to prevent tarnish from marking the skin or fabric. Before this ladies had to clean and brush their jewellery regularly. Close-backed settings were prevalent throughout most of the eighteenth century but settings with open backs, known as 'à jour', became preferable in the early nineteenth, because of the proliferation of the brilliant cut diamond.

Left:
Imperial topaz open backed rivière with pendent cross set in gold c.1820

Below:
19th century cushion cut open backed diamond rivière set in silver and gold c.1820

Above:
Rose cut diamond rivière and earrings closed-set in silver and gold c.1800

Right:
Detail of reverse of rose cut closed back diamond rivière above

Opposite:
Rainbow of Georgian paste rivières, foiled and set in gold, swagged beneath a pavé diamond and foiled topaz heart pendant

Rivières of paste or coloured precious and semi-precious stones set in gold were also highly effective. They were frequently made with detachable matching pendants and were usually foiled unless the stones were of such a quality as to not require it.

Unlike more intricate necklaces, fabulous examples of rivières seem to have escaped the fate of being broken up and redesigned, perhaps because they were so enduringly lovely they never went out of style.

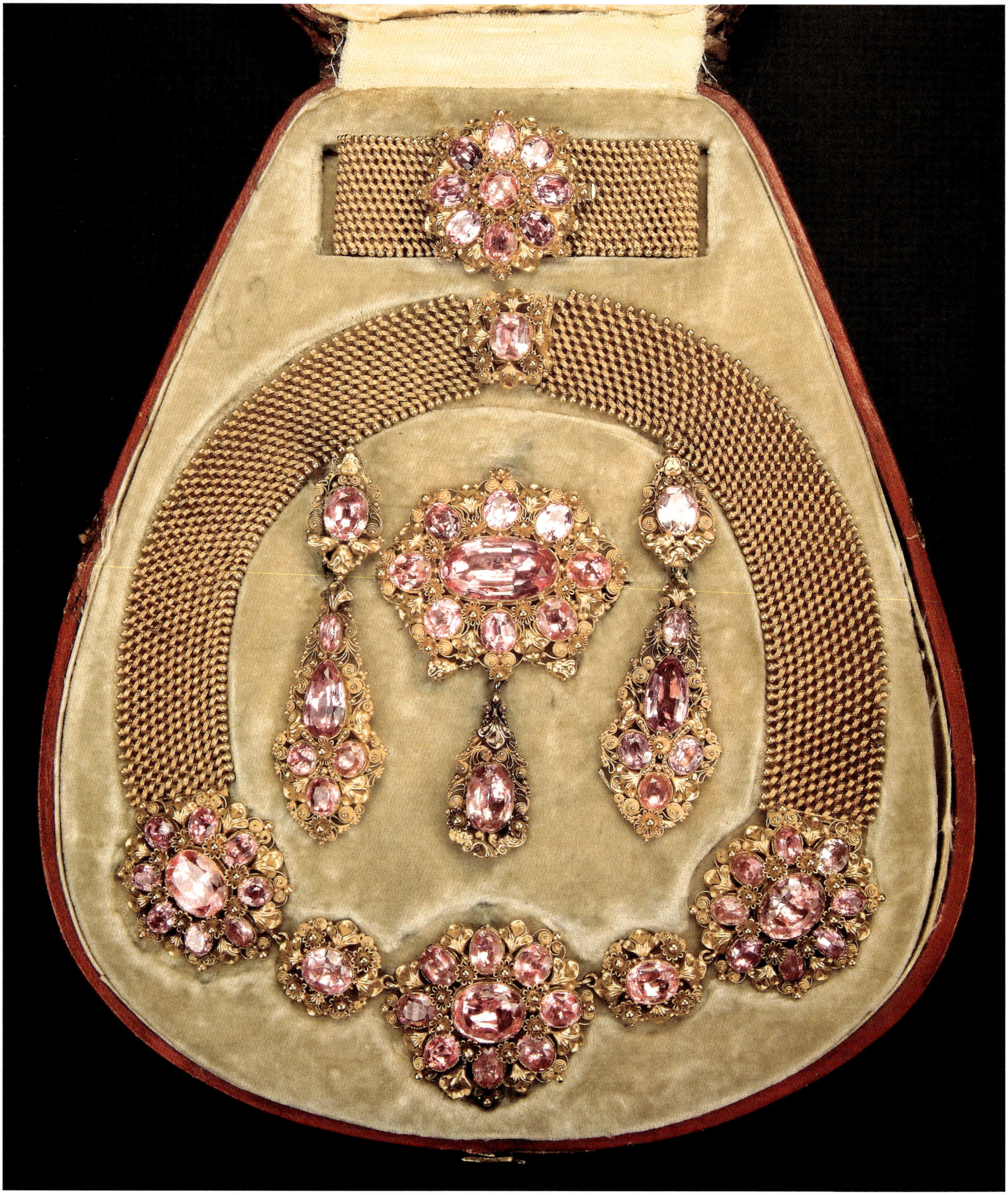

Boxed pink topaz and gold cannetille parure c.1820

Boxed aquamarine and gold cannetille parure c.1820

The parure

Formal eighteenth century jewellery was very often made in parures: boxed jewels of uniform design set with matching stones. These could be had in small sets, called demi-parures, containing as little as two pieces (necklace and earrings) or three (necklace, earrings, and brooch). But when it came to night-time jewellery, wealthy women might own an extensive parure with as many as sixteen matching pieces all beautifully arrayed in an enormous satin-lined leather box. These boxes might contain a necklace, earrings, hair ornaments, dress ornaments (such as bows), a set of buttons, a waist buckle, a pair of bracelets, a pendant and some brooches. All of these would be made of matching diamonds, pearls or coloured stones and would have been designed to complement a particular lady's formal or court dress.

Closed-back silver-set rose cut diamond cross c.1750

Close-up of closed setting and open setting

Example of cut-down setting in diamond ring c.1770

The evolution of settings

The setting of diamonds and gemstones evolved from the closed settings of the seventeenth century – in which the complete underside of the stone from the girdle downwards is encased in metal (usually silver) – to the box settings of the eighteenth century in which the stone is encircled by a narrow band of metal, called a collet, and is left closed- or open-set depending on the quality of the stone. A refinement of the collet setting was the cut-down setting, in which the metal of the collet was castellated and cut or filed down to give the piece a finer, more finished appearance and helped make the settings airtight if they were foiled and closed-set. These earlier styles of settings were eventually supplanted by the claw and millegrained settings of the mid-nineteenth and twentieth centuries.

Foiling

Foiling was a method of enhancing gemstones in some of the most arresting jewellery of the Georgian period. While the finest stones could be set with open backs, others were put in closed settings with a sliver of foil underneath which brightened the diamonds and intensified the colours of gemstones. (It could also make a non-precious stone or a poorly-cut one look like a finely-cut precious gem.) Foils produced the magical depth which seemed to increase the refraction of light and draw the eye 'into' the stone for a rich and shimmering effect. Unlike the tinfoil of today, the reflective material was a rigid piece of copper tinted to the required colour, or silvered for diamonds. Over time these foils tended to fade, or slightly tarnish, but often this has only added to the ephemeral beauty of the piece.

18th century foiled topaz rivière, crowned heart Portuguese ring and pendeloque earrings

Foiled amethyst and gold swag necklace and earrings c.1820

Back of pink topaz and diamond cross showing the combination of open and closed settings

Maltese cross with open-backed pink topazes and closed-back diamonds, 2¼in. long, c.1825

Slides, brooches and pendants

Great quantities of diamonds and gemstones were used in the making of important brooches, pendants and slides in Georgian times. Slides had two vertical struts across the back of the piece through which to thread a ribbon. The ribbon would be long enough to be tied at the nape of the neck. Bows, with or without crosses or drops, were the motifs most often seen. Pendants also usually took the form of crosses or bow-drops and were worn on chain, velvet ribbon or attached to rivières. Brooches, which could be larger and asymmetrical, assumed a greater variety of figural designs, such as feathers, leaves, daisies, crowns, floral bouquets and cornucopias. The most extravagant of these might have articulated diamond pendent drops or even a detachable descending series of them.

Foiled rose diamond pavé-set bow slide, closed-set in silver c.1760

Old cut closed-set diamond leaf brooch c.1820 and girandole brooch c.1810

18th century diamond cluster brooch in the form of a cornucopia with floral and foliate display, closed-set in silver and gold c.1760

Opposite above:
Spanish silver-set ruby and diamond floral and foliate necklace c.1720 with ruby and diamond earrings of a slightly later date

Opposite below:
Emerald and diamond bow-drop necklace c.1790

Below:
French boxed diamond, emerald and ruby necklace c.1820 with Spanish brooch and earrings c.1750

Precious gems with diamonds

During the early part of the Georgian era, small necklets, like the ribbon-tie choker, dominated evening wear but, in the later years, these were superseded by necklaces constructed on a grander scale. As fashions changed, the décolleté of ball gowns revealed an ever-widening area of exposed flesh which brought about the demand for ever more opulent jewellery. By the time of the Regency period (1810-1830), diamonds, when they were not set as fabulous necklaces on their own, had become accents for precious gemstones such as rubies, emeralds and sapphires for full-dress occasions. Often a necklace would display large coloured gemstones in wide settings. The more expensive of these would have diamond borders and were linked together by smaller matching stones. These links would sometimes support pear-shaped pearls or drops of the same colour that radiated outwards. Necklaces such as these were worn low and wide on the neck and shoulders to fill in the broad expanse of décolletage.

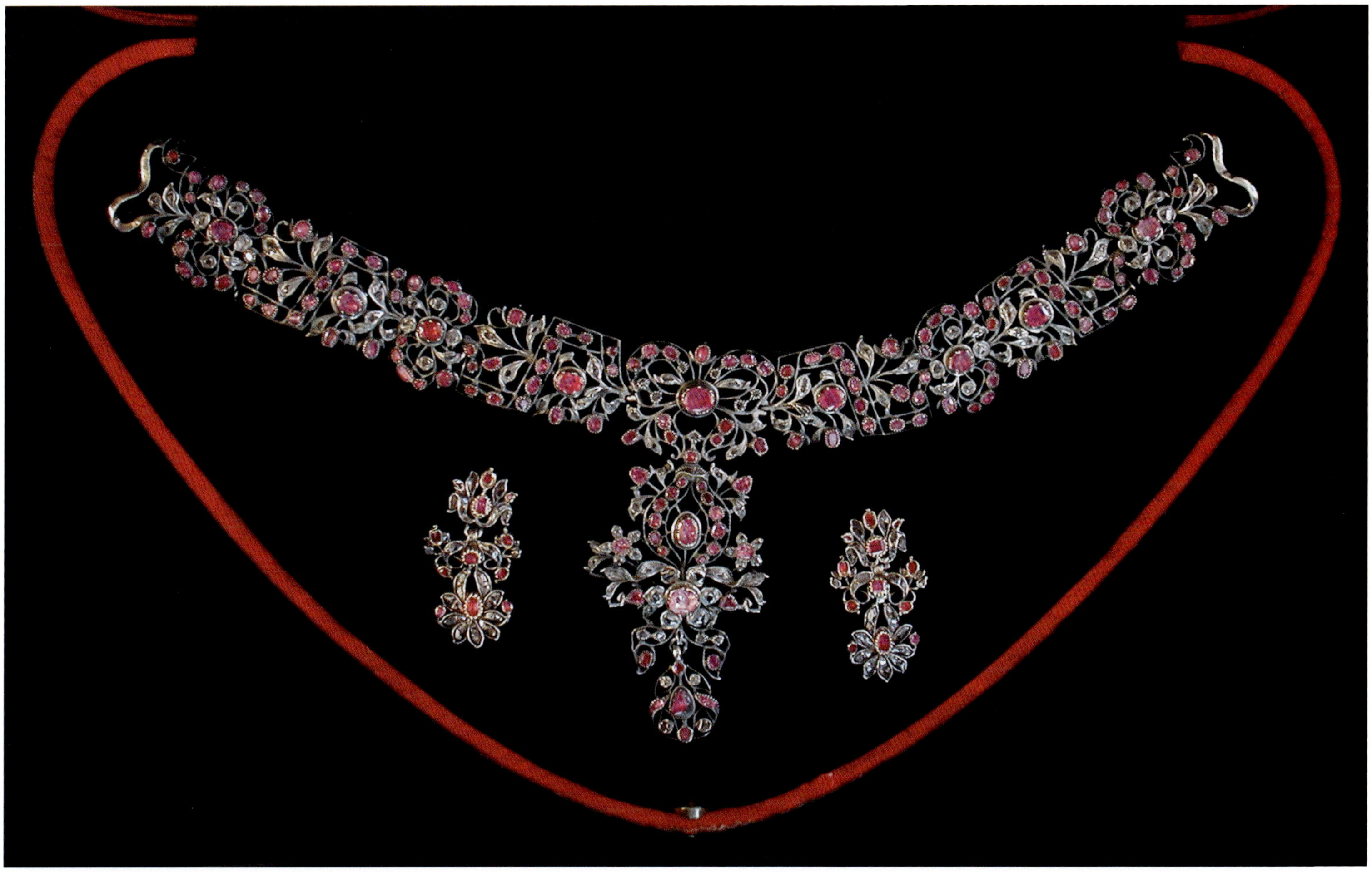

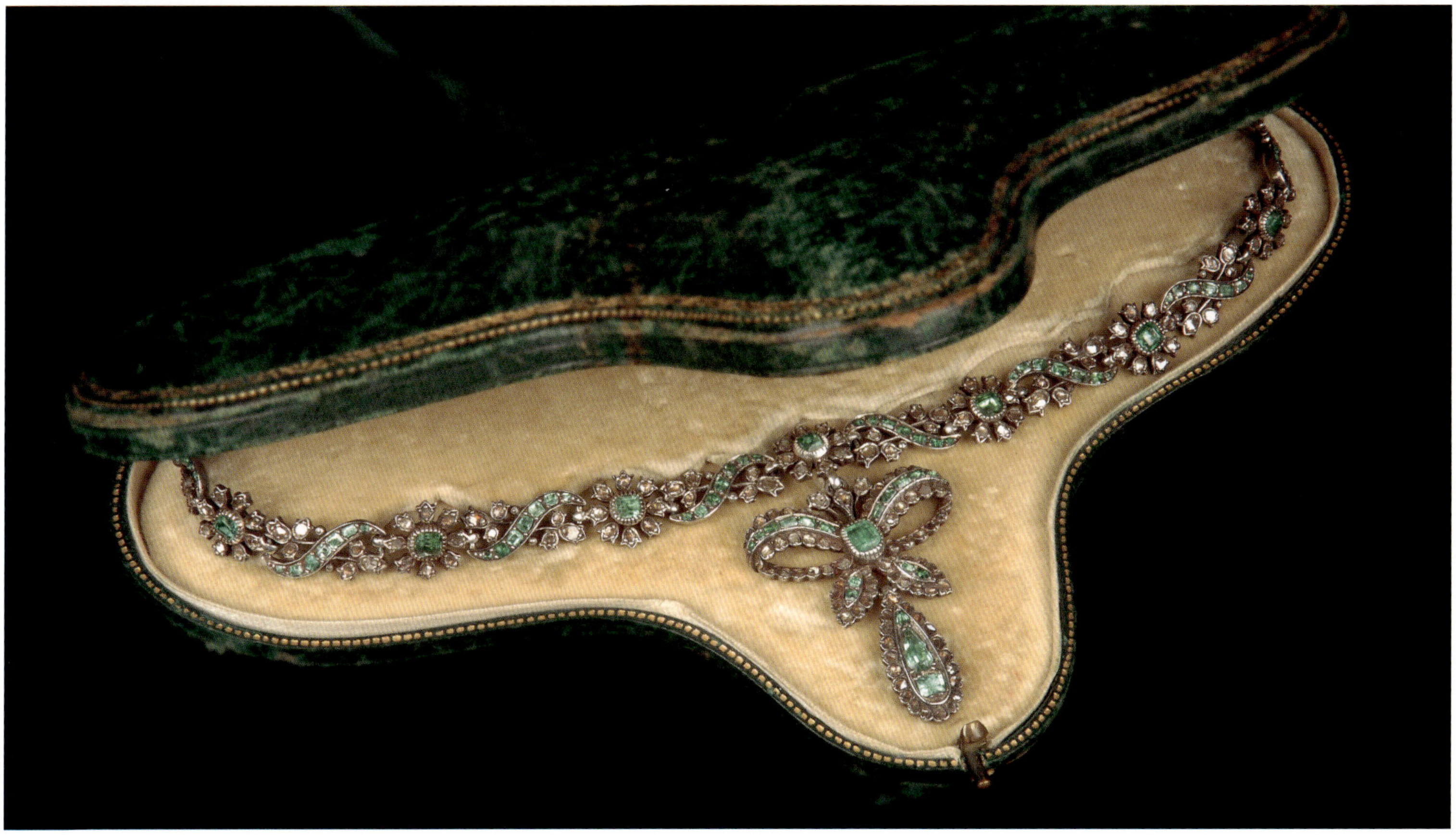

Above:
Early 19th century sapphire and diamond rings, earrings and necklace set in silver and gold

Left:
Foiled emerald and old cut diamond drop earrings c.1820

Opposite:
Regency period multi-gemstone drop necklace c.1820 with mid-19th century diamond butterfly brooch

Above:
Five-stone rose cut diamond half-hoop ring with multiple basket settings c.1800

Above:
Large pink topaz cigar band ring w/diamond surround c.1830

Below:
Large foiled moonstone ring with diamond surround c.1830

Rings

Around 1830, a footman in the service of the widow of a city businessman described some of her friends playing cards at a party 'dressed up monsterous *[sic]* fine with their jewellery. I took notice of whow *[sic]* many rings were on the fingers of four of these old cats, as I call them, and there were no less than thirty-one, some wedding, some mourning, and others set with diamonds and precious stones of great value'.

Rings of the eighteenth century took every shape and form from octagonal and marquise, to square, oval and circular with wide shoulders and shanks of carved flowers and leaves. Diamonds and precious coloured stones were often framed with a surround of tiny diamonds or were flanked on each shoulder by a pair of brilliants. Hoops or half hoops set with diamonds, pearls or coloured stones could be worn in groupings or might be designed as a double or triple row. Foiled rings of high quality often had fluted 'basket' settings underneath to enclose the foil and give the stone a much-needed appearance of depth. Large single-stone or two-stone specimen rings were rare, especially when set with diamonds, rubies, emeralds or sapphires. Many rings with big centre stones used gems that were semi-precious, or paste. Cluster rings of smaller diamonds, densely packed, were more usual and looked expensive and dramatic without the exacting the price of a large single stone ring. Finely-carved shanks could also be very persuasive in increasing the importance of less than stellar stones.

Opposite:

Top:
Large single-stone rose cut diamond ring with Russian royal provenance c.1800

Centre:
Fine emerald and diamond rings: left, early 19th century; right, late 18th

Below left:
Pavé-set rose diamond ring with cigar band shank c.1820

Below centre:
Foiled large rose cut diamond ring with swagged shank c.1800

Below right:
Open-set old cut diamond flower ring c.1820

Opposite:
Multicoloured gemstone pansy necklace with detachable drop c.1790

Below:
Harlequin foiled gemstone brooches and necklace c.1820

Harlequin jewels

'Harlequin' was the adjective used to describe the fashion for combining dissimilar but complementary coloured stones in necklaces, bracelets, earrings, brooches and rings in the late eighteenth and early nineteenth centuries. Colourful and attractive, harlequin jewels were usually foiled and were sometimes set with pastes rather than gemstones. The most delightful harlequin jewels have been designed in the shapes of flowers, sometimes as pansies, with lovely aquamarines, amethysts and topazes imitating the colours of the petals.

Opposite:
Foiled white paste necklace, earrings and brooch with large rock crystal drop, early 19th century

Right:
White paste earrings set in silver, Portuguese c.1780

Below:
Boxed silver and paste ribbon tie choker with bow and drop c.1770

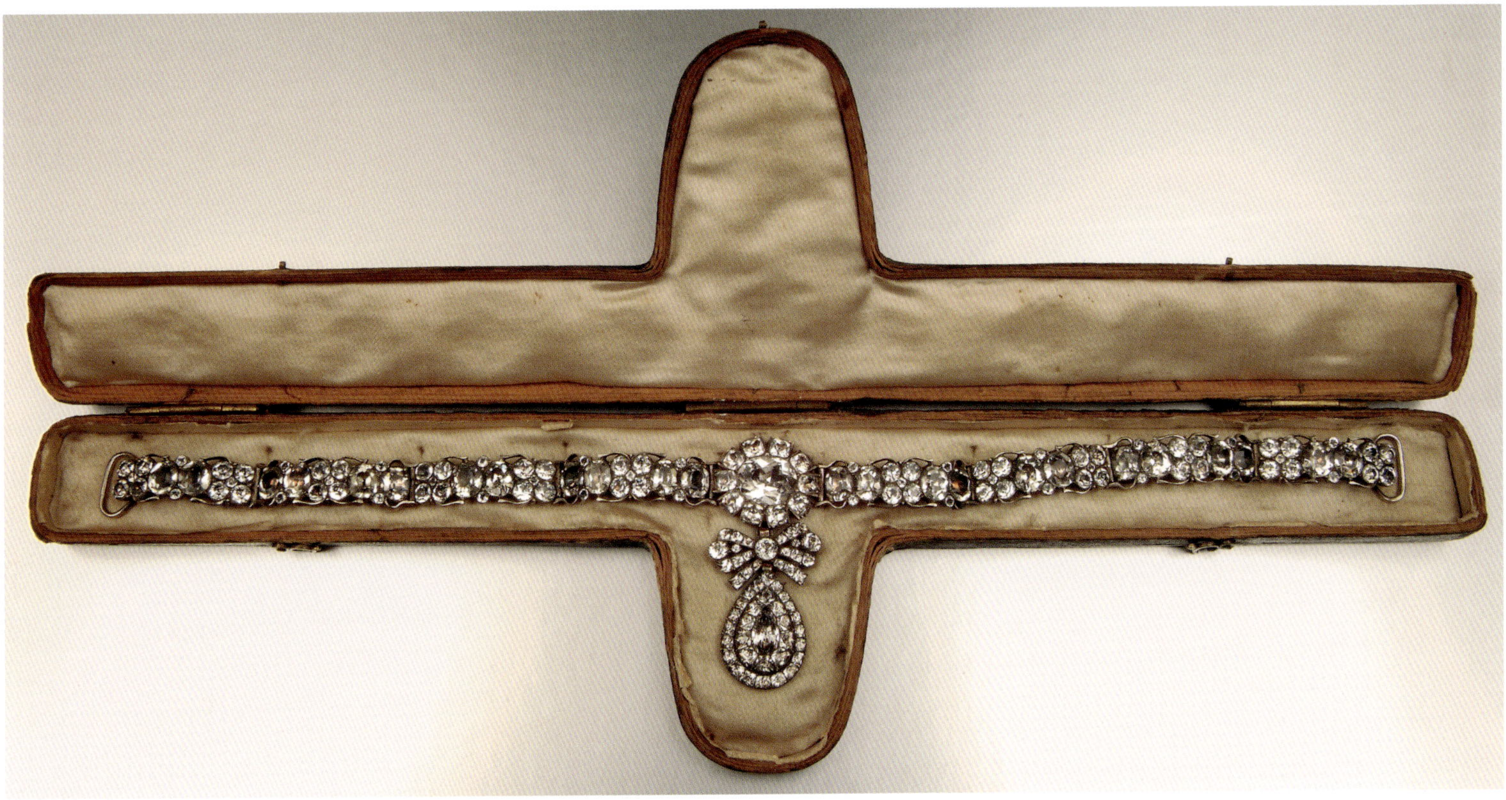

Paste

Glass had been used to imitate gemstones from the earliest days of adornment but paste is one of the great joys of the seventeenth and eighteenth centuries. Pastes were not seen as faux gems made solely to copy, but as exciting jewels in their own right. The care and workmanship that went into the best pieces produced glorious jewellery that would have shone at the greatest of occasions, and fine paste is coveted by the collectors of today. Unlike diamonds – where size matters – the stones could be cut into any shape required which meant that the setting (usually of silver) could be almost invisible. The stones would also be foiled to add extra brilliance and further catch and reflect light.

'Queen Anne' amethyst paste necklace and earrings set in gilt metal c.1750

In 1675 George Ravenscroft developed a hard lead glass which was very popular, as did the firm of Wickes and Netherton soon after. In 1734, M. Georges-Frédéric Stras of Paris added a high content of lead to his paste and the result was a brilliant and hard stone which could take a high polish: the eponymous 'stras'. Fashionable ladies everywhere began embracing these faux alternatives and suddenly relatively affordable finery could shine at dinners and dances, infusing the whirl of Georgian society with a kaleidoscope of richness and colour.

'Queen Anne' jewellery (misleadingly named, as it was made in the mid-eighteenth century rather than during the reign of Queen Anne – 1695-1714), was ideally suited to the properties of paste. The necklaces were usually non-graduated rivières mounted in gilt metal, and their vibrant collet-set pastes were faceted as rose cuts. A distinctively shaped oval removable pendent drop frequently hung suspended from the centre stone. 'Queen Anne' earrings were chunky looking, with thick back-to-front fittings. These were worn very close to the earlobe and most often consisted of two oblong pastes (the lower one slightly larger than the upper) soldered together with smaller stones flanking the conjoined area.

Opposite:
Pavé-set paste earrings, bracelet clasp and Celtic crowned harp brooch in silver and gold c.1790

While paste was perfect for creating marvellous hues that did not occur in nature, many pieces were made to replicate genuine gems as there was great fear among those fortunate enough to own diamonds and precious stones of their being lost or stolen by street robbers or highwaymen while travelling. Paste was a particularly suitable diamond replacement and early to mid-eighteenth century pieces usually have a black dot in the centre to imitate the culets of old cut diamonds which enhanced their depth.

Another material used to simulate diamonds in eighteenth century jewellery was rock crystal, a natural, colourless transparent quartz that can be distinguished from paste by its greater hardness, coldness and double refraction

Opposite:
Selection of fine emerald paste set in gold c.1800

Right:
Daisy brooches in paste or diamonds: left: red and white paste; right: top, paste; left, diamonds; right, paste

Below:
Left, diamond 'cornucopia' earrings; right, single paste earring and rose diamond 'snap' earrings– all late 18th century

Silver and rock crystal pendeloque earrings, 4in. (10cm) long, in original box, c.1780

(although it lacks the fire of diamonds). Within this category are the rose cut crystals from Bristol, called bristowes, that were used to great effect in English and Flemish jewellery.

Cut-steel

There are few diamond substitutes more effective than cut-steel and none more unlikely, considering the material from which it was made – the horseshoe nails that littered the muddy lanes of enterprising English villages in the eighteenth century.

Cut-steel jewellery is comprised of tiny studs mounted into base plates. Although steel work is said to date back possibly to Elizabethan times, it first

Opposite:
Cut steel parure of early work c.1785, possibly made in Tula, Russia

Fine cut-steel necklace c.1800

Long cut-steel bow drop earrings c.1820

became a lucrative cottage industry in the mid-1700s situated in the little Oxfordshire village of Woodstock which specialised in the making of chatelaines, watch chains, scissors, and sword hilts. As the demand for cut-steel jewellery grew in both England and France, Birmingham, under the supervision of industrialist Matthew Boulton, began manufacturing quantities

Cut-steel fringe necklace with foliate earrings c.1820

of cut-steel buttons and jewellery in the late 1700s. By using women as cheap labour, Birmingham eventually overshadowed Woodstock and continued to be the primary source of cut-steel until it went out of style in the last quarter of the 1800s. Although no one seems to know how much jewellery was made in Woodstock, it is generally believed that Woodstock's work was superior to Birmingham's; it was certainly more expensive. There is a record of a pair of steel scissors there costing fifteen guineas (British gold coins worth over £1 each, from 1717 fixed at 21s. – £1.1s.) in 1778!

Making cut-steel jewellery was difficult and time-consuming. First the steel nails or studs were individually faceted and polished. The studs were then individually riveted through tiny holes in a base plate usually made of brass or low-grade silver. The studs were faceted and mounted in such a way as to catch as much light as possible and provide a brilliance not unlike that of diamonds. Very ornate examples had more than one base plate to give the piece dimension; these plates were affixed to each other by tiny steel supports on the

underside. If a piece had a centre medallion, it was usually mobile. One can distinguish the pieces that are made of individual studs simply by turning them over and noticing the lack of uniformity in the rivets. Later, the mass production of cut-steel – in which studs were stamped out in ribbon-like sheets rather than individually riveted – caused its decline.

There has been a tendency to categorise most cut-steel as eighteenth century, but this is erroneous. Cut-steel was never signed, but early pieces were often heavier in weight and appearance as many of them were made with a secondary solid plate reinforcing the base-plate. Because the shoe buckle declined in the late 1700s, one can assume that most cut-steel shoe buckles date from prior to this period, as do many other trinkets such as chatelaines. In later eighteenth century pieces the studs tended to be smaller and more densely packed than the ones of the Victorian era. The best early pieces had as many as fifteen facets per stud (whereas most Victorian pieces had five facets) and one sees the use of a variety of different sized studs to create a more brilliant effect. Earlier necklaces often had graduated drops, rosettes or garlands rather than uniform ones. Sometimes it is possible to date pieces by their subject matter, since the same themes that were fashionable in contemporary precious jewellery prevailed in cut-steel. While it continued to be made until the end of the nineteenth century in England and well into the twentieth century in France, the quality and workmanship of these later pieces was rarely as fine or innovative.

Detail of back of the cut-steel necklace

Opposite:
Important cut-steel necklace, early 19th century

Right:
Blinded by the Light! – cut-steel button cartoon

Portrait by unknown artist of Catherine the Great wearing cut-steel parure

Unusual iron pyrites ribbon-tie necklace cut to simulate rose cut diamonds c.1740

Cut-steel became fashionable in France in 1759 when wealthy people, who were asked to donate their jewels to the treasury, began wearing cut-steel instead. Much of what Birmingham made in the mid-1700s was exported to France until a Yorkshireman named Sykes moved to Paris in 1780 and began a cut-steel industry there. By the late eighteenth century cut-steel had become big business, and Frenchmen such as Deferney and Frichot had thriving enterprises. Frichot was best known for his sizable parures in floral motifs. A most celebrated Parisian boutique was Au Petit Dunkerque, owned by a Monsieur Granchez, Marie Antoinette's jeweller. It was here that jewellery made of cut-steel could command higher prices than equivalent gold pieces. Even Napoleon was not blind to the brilliance of cut-steel; he bought Empress Marie Louise an impressive parure from Deferney. Catherine the Great of Russia was a true enthusiast and was painted in the late 1700s wearing an enormous parure of cut-steel with tiara, stomacher and massive necklace with great rounded plaques and a crown motif pendent drop.

It is hard to find great examples of cut-steel jewellery today because much of it has succumbed to a cruel fate: rust in the face of dampness. But when they appear, they are prized by many collectors.

Iron pyrites and marcasites

Cut-steel is very often confused with marcasite jewellery because both possess a similar grey metallic sheen, but marcasites are made of iron pyrites, a natural mineral, and are set like diamonds rather than riveted. At first, pyrites and marcasites were used to imitate diamonds, but evolved into being appreciated for their intrinsic steely beauty. They were also used to great effect as the surrounds for enamels or miniatures on ivory, or faceted crystal pieces.

Coque de perle *and iron pyrites bow drop earrings c.1760*

Earrings

Of all the styles of eighteenth century earrings, the girandole was probably the most desirable for night wear. Its design was classic: a central bow-shaped ornament from which were suspended three pear-shaped pendants, the middle pendant usually larger than the two flanking it. Dating back to the seventeenth century, when beautiful examples were made in rose cut diamonds, the girandole remained fashionable for over a hundred years, possibly because the proportion was particularly flattering to the female face. During the eighteenth century girandoles were produced all over Europe in every conceivable material, but some of the most fabulous were crafted in Portugal of topaz and chrysoberyl.

White paste and silver Portuguese girandole earrings c.1770

When girandoles finally went out of fashion, many outstanding examples were broken up but, later on, the smaller pear-shaped drops often reappeared as earrings and, frequently, the central part was reborn as a pendant.

The other essential earring for night was the bow-drop earring called the pendeloque. It was characterised by a top (either round or marquise-shaped) connected to a figural bow supporting a drop usually of a similar design to the top. Its outline was often elongated and slightly exaggerated, probably to offset the extremely high hairstyles of the 1770s.

Chrysoberyl silver-set pendeloque earrings with gold beading c.1760

Many variations have since sprung from the design of the earliest pendeloques: the shorter round topped/central bow/oval pendent earring, and the simple bow topped pendent earring which eventually evolved into the two-stone earring (a smaller stone connected to a larger one) that has remained in style ever since. Not many early pendeloques have survived, the metal having been melted down and the gems reset by subsequent owners.

Fittings for earrings of the eighteenth century showed tremendous ingenuity. The back-to-front fitting, which was inserted through the back of a pierced earlobe and snapped into place at the front, was the most frequent method of attachment. Many of these were later converted to the simpler 'shepherd's hook' fitting, which was inserted, more easily, from the front. In 1773 a new mechanism was made whereby a woman could attach her earrings to her ears without having them pierced. These were called 'snaps' and are the

Left:
Silver-set early green and white paste drop earrings

Right:
Early silver and rose cut diamond drop earrings c.1740

Left:
Back of the green and white paste drop earrings showing the original fittings, Portugal c.1750

Left:
Emerald and diamond cornucopia earrings c.1770

Right:
Silver-set rose cut diamond and garnet earrings c.1770

precursors of modern 'clip-ons'. The problem of the heaviness of the girandole with its three drops was addressed by adding a fine hook of silver or silk to go over the ear and support the earring. Even so, ladies' ears suffered greatly.

Historically, large earrings have come and gone in fashion although a book on jewellery written in 1905 by Cyril Davenport confidently reports: 'In England the ladies of the early Victorian period wore large earrings; mostly of diamonds; but the fashion has been slowly dying out ever since. I should think it is unlikely to be revived, although there have been some attempts in that direction'. (Dear deluded Mr. Davenport!)

Portuguese style pendant/brooch in amethyst paste, 19th century

Portuguese style pendant/brooch in aquamarine paste, 19th century

Foiled topaz poissarde earrings with gold beaded edges c.1800

Foiled Portuguese topaz flower brooches c.1760

Portuguese and Spanish jewellery

Both Portugal and Spain had colonies in South America. Brazil was a treasure trove of precious stones, yielding huge quantities of diamond, topaz, aquamarine and chrysoberyl gems, which were made into jewellery back in Portugal. These gemstones were pieced together and pavé-set to create suites of swagged and be-ribboned necklaces and earrings in floral and bow motifs. Portugal's production ran the gamut from large girandole earrings with matching pendant/brooches in precious stones or paste to diminutive flower brooches and hair ornaments of coloured stones that were set 'en tremblant'. This period of outstanding jewellery came to an abrupt halt with the French invasion of Portugal in 1809 – the Court fled and the country was plunged into war. Jewellery manufacture did not really recommence until the 1830s and the tendency was to create much the same styles as fifty years before, although the quality was not as fine.

Above left:
Spanish gold and emerald lazo drop earrings c.1760

Above right:
Catalan emerald and gold long drop earrings, c.1780

Spain had dominion over the emerald mines of Peru and Colombia and the richly coloured gold from the same area made Spain wealthy beyond her dreams. Finely wrought, pierced gold and emerald parures of necklaces, stomachers, rings and earrings were worn by nobility at the Spanish court. The earrings were variations on the basic design of top, bow and drop, and are frequently accompanied by the long ribbon-shaped bodice ornament called a 'lazo' (Spanish for bow). Classically Spanish are the distinctive gold and gem-set Iberian and Catalan earrings. They are often extremely long and traditionally set with emeralds or hessonite garnets. Amazingly, emerald and gold pieces are still being retrieved from the wrecks of Spanish galleons resting on the ocean beds and these pieces are as fresh as if they were made yesterday – three hundred years old and never worn!

Catalan long hessonite garnet and gold earrings c.1780

Portuguese chrysoberyl necklace, earrings and ring c.1760

Pink topaz

In 1735 the mines of Minas Gerais in Brazil yielded a seam of imperial topaz with a slight pinkish hue. A Parisian jeweller named Dumelle discovered that golden topaz became a glorious pink upon being heated and 'pinked' topaz became popular. The colourful floral and bow jewellery of Portugal made great use of this delightful gemstone, mixing it with chrysoberyl or aquamarine for the prettiest effect. Imperial topaz was always a costly gemstone and it is surprising how keen the lapidaries were to heat the stones. The trace element chromium is what created the pink colour upon heating, but not all imperial topaz contained this element. Topaz without chromium will become colourless and can easily fracture when heated. Possibly this explains the brief vogue for pink topaz, as it was not used so much in the following years of the nineteenth century. (There is a new deposit of natural pink-to-purplish topaz recently discovered in Pakistan. We shall see if the fashion is revived.)

Chrysoberyl

Another important gemstone used to great advantage in Portugal was chrysoberyl set in silver and fashioned into close-fitting, pavé-set necklaces, long earrings and navette-shaped rings with gold beaded decoration. The sparkling greenish-yellow stones are a uniquely compelling colour, subtle but powerful and very flattering to olive skin tones. Sometimes called Brazilian chrysolite, this gemstone was much in demand towards the last quarter of the eighteenth century.

Opposite:
Magnificent foiled imperial topaz parure, Portugal c.1760

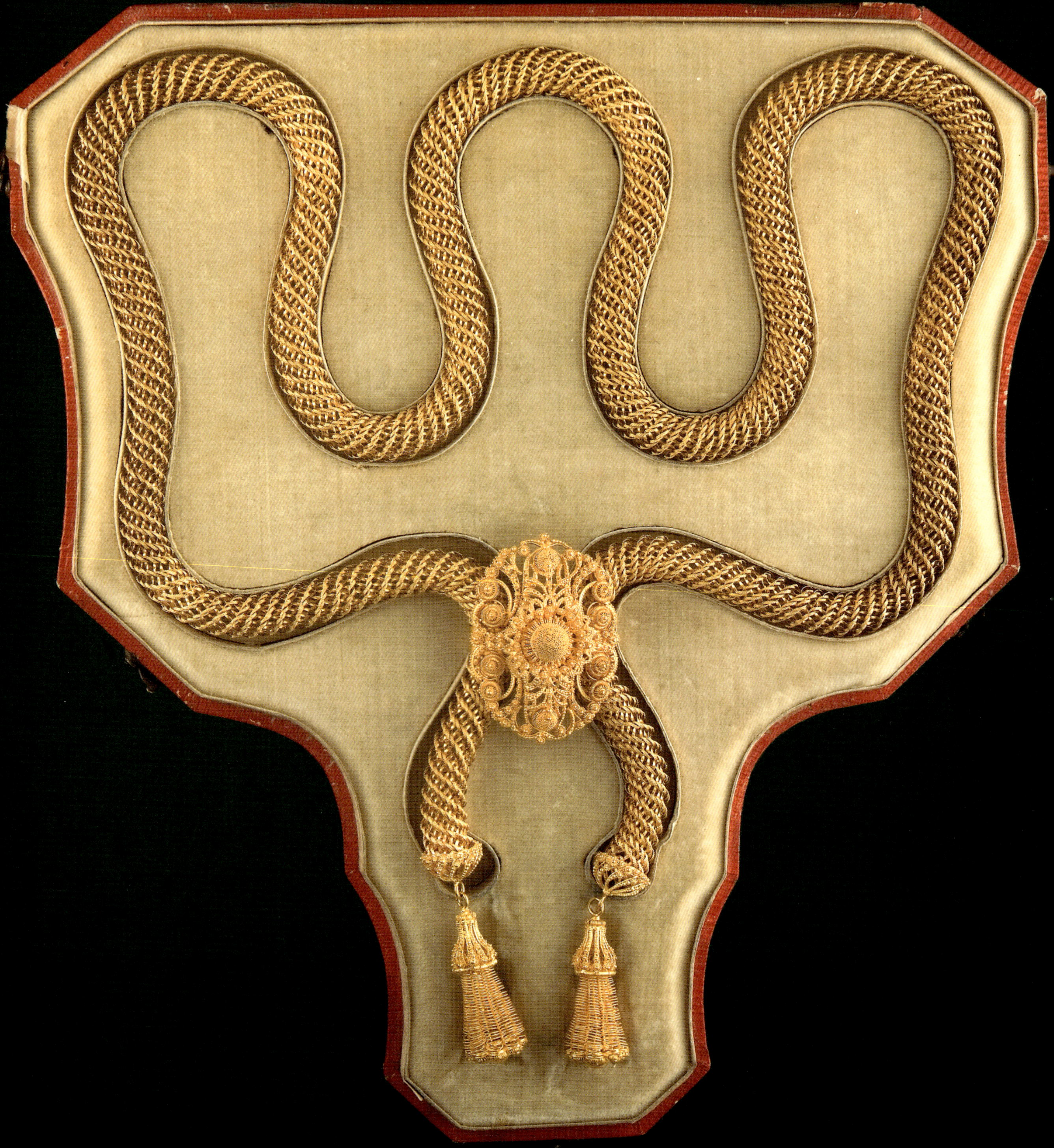

Gold meshwork and amethyst boxed parure c.1820

Gold evening jewellery

At the end of the 1700s, gold jewellery enjoyed a resurgence in desirability. Throughout the century it had been used for chatelaines, neck chains and watches and as the metal in which most precious jewellery (except for diamonds) was set. But, around 1780, pierced filigreed gold work was used to pleasing effect in regional France and in 1790, in England, a new technique of gold work called cannetille was destined to change dramatically the proportion of gemstones to gold in jewellery for years to come.

Cannetille work has highly intricate coils and tendrils of gold wire on a filigreed base forming tiny rosettes and loops to imitate the fine gold lace of the time. Unbelievably labour intensive (workmanship was relatively cheap), the gold was stretched into elaborate and complicated designs which also were light on gold content. Work such as this can never be cost effective again. A remarkable amount has survived – for all its ethereal appearance it is surprisingly strong although care must obviously be taken when handling it. The finest pieces are often set with relatively large foiled pink topazes and aquamarines in remarkable parures whose shimmering beauty sets off the fine tracery of the gold work.

Amethyst is another gemstone that lent itself beautifully to cannetille jewellery. Its rich, velvety foiled colour was the perfect complement for the

Opposite:
Fine 18ct woven chain with tassels in original box c.1800

Right:
Finely worked gold long drop earrings c.1820

Far right:
18ct gold and turquoise long drop earrings c.1830

intense eighteen carat yellow gold. Cannetille parures, while all the rage, were not universally admired or correct for all evening occasions. In 1806, a Miss Mitford tells of meeting rich Mrs. Beaumont wearing a cannetille necklace, bandeau, tiara, cestus, armlets, bracelets, brooches and shoe knots all set with large amethysts: 'All these she wore and I must confess, for a small dinner party, appeared rather too gaily decorated'.

Gold cannetille work and turquoise-set quizzer c.1830

Pink topaz, emerald and two-colour gold cannetille parure c.1830

Three-colour gold cannetille work bracelet with multicoloured gemstones c.1810

Important transitional en tremblant *pink topaz parure of cannetille and répoussé gold work, probably having belonged to a member of French aristocracy – ten pieces in original tooled leather box, France c.1830s*

Three French pink topaz and gold en tremblant *floral bouquet brooches that can be assembled to make a tiara, a stomacher or a shoulder ornament (part of the ten piece parure)*

Above:
View of the en tremblant *spring coils of the individual pieces*

Below:
The above pieces assembled to make a tiara

Gemstone bouquets

Evening jewels in the shape of flowers were a passion with Georgian women. T.D. Saint's *New Book of Designs for Jeweller's Work* published in 1770 contained over twenty plates of various sized floral bouquets for hair, neck, ears, wrists and dress. These became a speciality of the esteemed jeweller, James Cox, who exhibited them in 1774 in his catalogue. There he proclaims that his flowers were 'copied from nature in all its infinite variety of tints and forms with different

Above:
Rose cut diamond giardinetti brooch c.1780

Left:
Diamond pansy brooch of highest quality, possibly made by Court Jewellers Rundell, Bridge and Rundell c.1820

coloured gems – all in motion being fixed to springs of tempered gold which gives them vibrations as if blown by the wind…'. Though his might have been the finest bouquets, they were not the first. Giardinetti (little garden) brooches and rings had been made in Italy from the late seventeenth century and these were the precursors to the large bouquets *en tremblant* of the the late eighteenth. The bride in the play *The Clandestine Marriage* (1766) had these lines to perform: 'I have a bouquet to come home tomorrow, made up of diamonds and rubies, and emeralds and topazes, and amethysts – jewels of all colours, green, red, blue, yellow intermixt – the prettiest thing you ever saw in your life'.

Opposite:
Extraordinary Russian Royal jewels, made c.1750-60. A diadem and matching earrings depicting flowers and bees made of coloured diamonds with leaves of enamel. A bouquet brooch of coloured diamonds and emeralds and a narcissus brooch of coloured diamonds and enamel

Three enamel and diamond rings c.1790

Opposite:
Blue enamel and rose diamond chatelaine similar to one owned by the Duke of Devonshire, reputedly made for the Duke of Wellington to commemorate his being made a viscount in 1809; also a collection of rings and brooches of similar work, English and French 1780-1820

A faux enamel ring with a bezel of blue fabric under glass and bouquet of seed pearls

A fine enamel and diamond 'bague de firmament'

Royal blue enamel

Enamelling was out of favour for a good deal of the eighteenth century – with certain exceptions such as the highlighting of mourning jewellery – but, in 1775, the expert London enameller, Jusen, perfected a distinctly English style of enamelling on jewellery, which was a smooth, dark, translucent midnight blue. It is believed that the profusion of items in this remarkable colour began as gifts given to royals by other royals and, indeed, this colour is often seen as the background of rings, brooches, watches and bracelets displaying royal ciphers and crowns. Noted in Fanny Burney's *Diary*, the Princess Royal, eldest daughter of George III, was given 'a blue enamel ring with a large diamond in the middle and set round with smaller ones' by her brother, Frederick, Duke of York, for her twenty-second birthday in 1788. A pair of diamond bracelets with centres of rose cut diamond royal ciphers on blue enamel was given by George III to Countess Howe in 1794. Like many other trends of 'anglomanie', this one caught on, especially in France, where rings made of midnight blue enamel and a scattering of diamonds were called 'bagues de firmament' (rings of the sky). These became fashionable with all classes, causing them to be produced in both enamel and cheaper substitutes, such as foiled paste and Bristol glass, with pearls substituting for the more expensive diamonds.

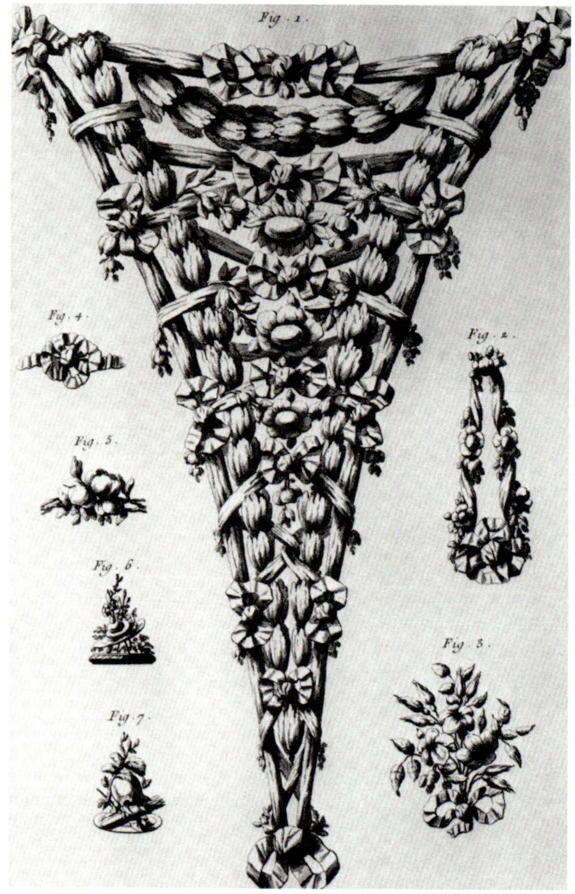

Above left:
Agate and gold vinaigrette c.1780

Above right:
Drawing of Madame du Barry's bodice ornament

Opposite:
Large blue paste and silver stomacher, 4½in. long, c.1770

Magnificent obsolescence

Some articles of eighteenth century jewellery may seem anachronistic today but cannot be overlooked because of their intrinsic loveliness and value and also for the very fact of their anachronism. While we are all familiar with the typical forms of jewellery, how many of us has ever seen a Georgian shoulder clasp or a girdle clasp or has ever had need for sleeve snaps, sleeve knots or a cestus? How many women use 'roses' (small gemstone flower pins) to hold their stays in place? How many women wear stays, for that matter? How many could benefit from a 'vinaigrette' – a wearable little container made to hold an aromatic preparation from which Georgian ladies could inhale as they walked the malodorous streets? No compendium on this era would be complete without mentioning the most interesting of these.

Some of the most delightful jewels of the eighteenth century were the sprays and bows and shuttles of diamonds and gemstones that were sewn on to ball gowns for full court dress. The Victoria and Albert Museum in London has a most beautiful collection of three sévigné bow brooches (so-named after the famous French letter writer, Madame de Sévigné) from the Russian royal collection made in 1760 in St. Petersburg of brilliant cut diamonds set in silver. Perfectly graduated, they would have been attached in descending order down the bodice of a gown. Covering that kind of expanse, it's no wonder Madame du Barry's diamond studded bodice, given her by Louis XV, was valued at a small fortune.

Stomachers were another kind of bodice jewel but these were oversized brooches (some of them over a foot, 30cm, long) made in several articulated sections to allow the wearer freedom of movement. The most extreme of these are an amazing concoction of gems in the shapes of flowers, foliage, ribbons and bow-knots cascading into an ever-narrowing V-shape and ending beyond the waist.

Old cut diamond sévigné brooch c.1790

Hair ornaments

The towering hairdos and wigs of the eighteenth century created the need for magnificent tiaras, bandeaux, diadems and coronets. These hair ornaments were studded with diamonds, dripping with pearls, and conceived in every imaginable motif from naturalistic flowers and vines to those that borrowed from antiquity using, among other designs, the Greek key and laurel wreath. At grand balls and soirées, twinkling cut-steel hair combs sat atop the heads of women and feathered plumes surrounded by brilliants bobbed and swayed in the candlelight. Asymmetrical jewelled aigrettes with dangling pendent drops perched upon fantastic hairdos and trembling gemstone flowers, butterflies, stars and comets peeked out and winked from the depths of white powdered wigs.

Above:
Cut-steel French wig pin

Right:
Flat cut garnet and gold aigrette c.1790

Opposite:
Selection of cut-steel tiaras, combs and hairpins c.1820

Silver and white paste tiara c.1820

Fine cut-steel hair ornament with pendent drops

Fashion magazines reported the ins and outs of head ornamentation. The June 1808 issue of *La Belle Assemblée* advised that 'the ornaments worn on the hair are alternately of diamonds, pearl or polished steel. Combs and coronets should be of silver filigree; bandeaux of pearls with a pear drop in the centre of the forehead'. Tiny jewelled flowers came into vogue in the 1770s and Lady Sarah Lawrence described the new French fashion: 'Hair must be powdered, curled in very small curls, and must be high and give your head the look of a sugar loaf ...little, little flowers dab'd in on the left side; the only feather permitted is a black or white sultane perched on the left side with your diamond feather against it'.

Jane Austen's sense of humour concerning the abuse of fashion is sharp in a letter to her sister Cassandra in 1800 when referring to an acquaintance whom she saw at a ball who 'appeared exactly as she did in September, with the same broad face, diamond bandeau, white shoes, pink husband and fat neck'! On a similar note, it was reported of a certain Lady Guidon: 'Her headdress is high, built up like a diamond and is so covered with jewels that they compare her to a lark wrapped in crumbs'.

Magnificent multi-gemstone cannetille and grainti tiara with precious gemstone cross c.1820

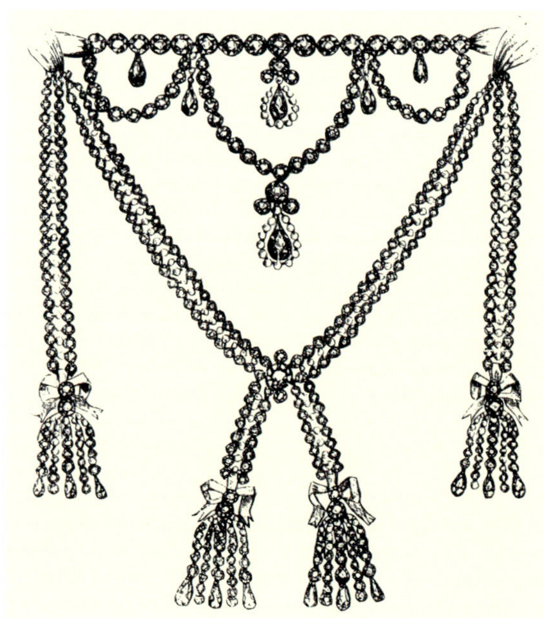

In 1807, a French ladies' magazine reported that an unnamed marchioness wore 'a rainbow coronet formed of diverse precious stones' to court. One can only imagine it being as dazzling as the one pictured above!

Right:
A rendering of the fated Queen's necklace

Opposite:
Portrait of Marie Antoinette by Jacques Gautier D'Agoty

Marie Antoinette and the affair of the necklace

Marie Antoinette had an unlucky reign which started with injustice and ended with the guillotine.

One of the most unfair incidents which contributed greatly to her downfall and subsequent execution was the 'Affair of the Diamond Necklace'. A spectacular diamond necklace was ordered by Louis XV for Madame du Barry from his jewellers, but he died before it was completed. It had 647 diamonds and cost the equivalent of a fully rigged warship. His successor, Louis XVI (Marie Antoinette's husband) considered it too expensive and refused to buy it. A plot was laid by a Madame de Saint-Rémy, the Comtesse de la Motte, who persuaded the Cardinal de Rohan that the Queen wished to buy the necklace without the King's knowledge and desired the Cardinal to negotiate the purchase. To curry favour with her, he obtained the necklace and handed it over to a trusted servant of the Queen, or so he believed. And then the necklace disappeared!

Finally, the jewellers asked the Queen to pay, and she, knowing nothing at all about it, realised she had been set up. She carefully watched to see who had betrayed her and eventually the whole intrigue was exposed. La Motte and the Cardinal stood trial and Marie Antoinette was exonerated but the 'Affair' cast her in a terrible light, and the public chose to misunderstand her part in it. Her popularity evaporated and her reputation as an extravagant spendthrift was set for posterity.

Multi gemstone pendant locket in gold bearing an exquisitely painted miniature of an 18th century woman, 2¼in. in length

Chapter 4

Love

The jewellery of the eighteenth century gives a strong indication of the values that were then embraced and the people who embodied them. It was a time of unabashed sentiment, romance and intrigue. It's surprising how pre-occupied with love the Georgians were, given that many of them were forced into pre-arranged marriages. But if they could not find love with their prescribed mate, they had no compunction about searching for it elsewhere. What we are now examining are the relics of a civilisation of true romantics (and lusty individuals) who made their feelings known by bestowing precious tokens on the objects of their affections.

18th century posy rings: left, 'In thee my choyce I do rejoyce'; right, 'Love for love'

The romance of rings

The great lexicographer, Dr. Samuel Johnson, defined a ring as: 'A circular instrument placed upon the noses of hogs and the fingers of women to restrain them and bring them into subjection'. His ironic wit notwithstanding, Dr. Johnson is known to have adored his wife and was devastated when she died. In fact, he kept her wedding ring in a box by his bedside for the rest of his life.

Some of the simplest and earliest sentimental rings were called 'posies' (derived from the words poesy or poetry). These are usually plain gold rings used as betrothal or marriage bands with a simple line of poetry such as 'God above increase our love' or 'While life doth last, I'll hold thee fast' and they are often decorated with ivy leaves (which stand for long lasting love). Posy rings had been used as love tokens since the fifteenth century and gradually began shedding their inscriptions in the eighteenth evolving into the un-inscribed gold wedding bands we wear today. The fourth finger of the left hand was traditionally (and erroneously) supposed to have a vein running straight to the heart.

Three ancient forms of rings are the Fede, the Gimmel and the Claddagh. The Fede ring (Italian for 'to trust') is a ring of two clasped hands which sometimes opens to show a third ring of entwined hearts. A Gimmel is a ring in two parts (gimmel from Gemellus – the twins), one of which would each be worn by the betrothed couple until joined in marriage when the rings would be re-united and placed on the bride's finger. The Claddagh ring has two hands holding a heart in the centre and can be of gold or silver or gems.

Opposite:
Portrait by Sir Joshua Reynolds of Lady Elizabeth Keppel. She and a companion are shown arranging a garland around a statue of Hymen, the god of marriage. The picture commemorates Lady Elizabeth's role as bridesmaid at the wedding of George III and Queen Charlotte in 1761.
By kind permission of
His Grace the Duke of Bedford and the Trustees of the Bedford Estates

Gold and enamel Fede ring c.1750 and detail of opened Fede ring

Inscription on sentimental ring c.1820

This style then evolved into a heart-shaped central stone with a more circular stone on either side. The central heart is often crowned with a tiny coronet or a bow. (Clasped hands were also often featured on the clasps of the long chains worn by ladies in the early part of the nineteenth century.)

Sentimental rings were frequently used as informal gifts between couples or special friends. These could have entwined ciphers spelling out the initials of the pair; or hold miniatures or silhouettes of a beloved; or bear inscriptions, sometimes in French, such as 'Doux et sincère', or 'The farther I fly the faster we tye' alluding to the theory that absence makes the heart grow fonder.

Exceptionally fine closed-back diamond ring c.1770

The diamond ring – all its facets

As the ultimate love token for betrothal and marriage, the diamond ring replaced the posy in the mid-eighteenth century and has never been out of favour since. Like today, there was no one example then that epitomised the ring that every woman desired – it was more a question of individual preference and economics. In quality, some of the finest of these rings might have held a large round or oval open-backed early brilliant cut diamond with smaller diamonds as embellishments to the shoulders. But, popular with all classes, they were made in all manner of shapes and sizes and set with rose cuts, table cuts, or even pastes. A 'keeper' (a forerunner to the eternity band) was usually worn with it in order to make sure the bigger ring was protected and could not slip off the finger. The keeper could be a plain gold, enamelled or gemstone-set band. George III gave Queen Charlotte just such a diamond band in 1761.

By the nineteenth century diamond rings were used most often for betrothal and became ever more varied, some with cushion, heart or navette-shaped central stones or more intricate arrangements of diamonds in clusters. The keeper evolved into the wedding band and its design escalated from the simple gold band to a single, double or triple hoop of diamonds or gemstones.

High quality open-set diamond cluster ring c.1800

Collection of gems-set bands early 19th century

Collection of rose cut diamond rings late 18th and early 19th century

Ruby, pearl and chrysoberyl heart pendant with cannetille work c.1825

Silver pavé-set diamond arrow brooch c.1820

Multi-gemstone padlock pendant c.1810

Blue enamel and gold snake ring with rose cut diamond head and flexible segmented body c.1830

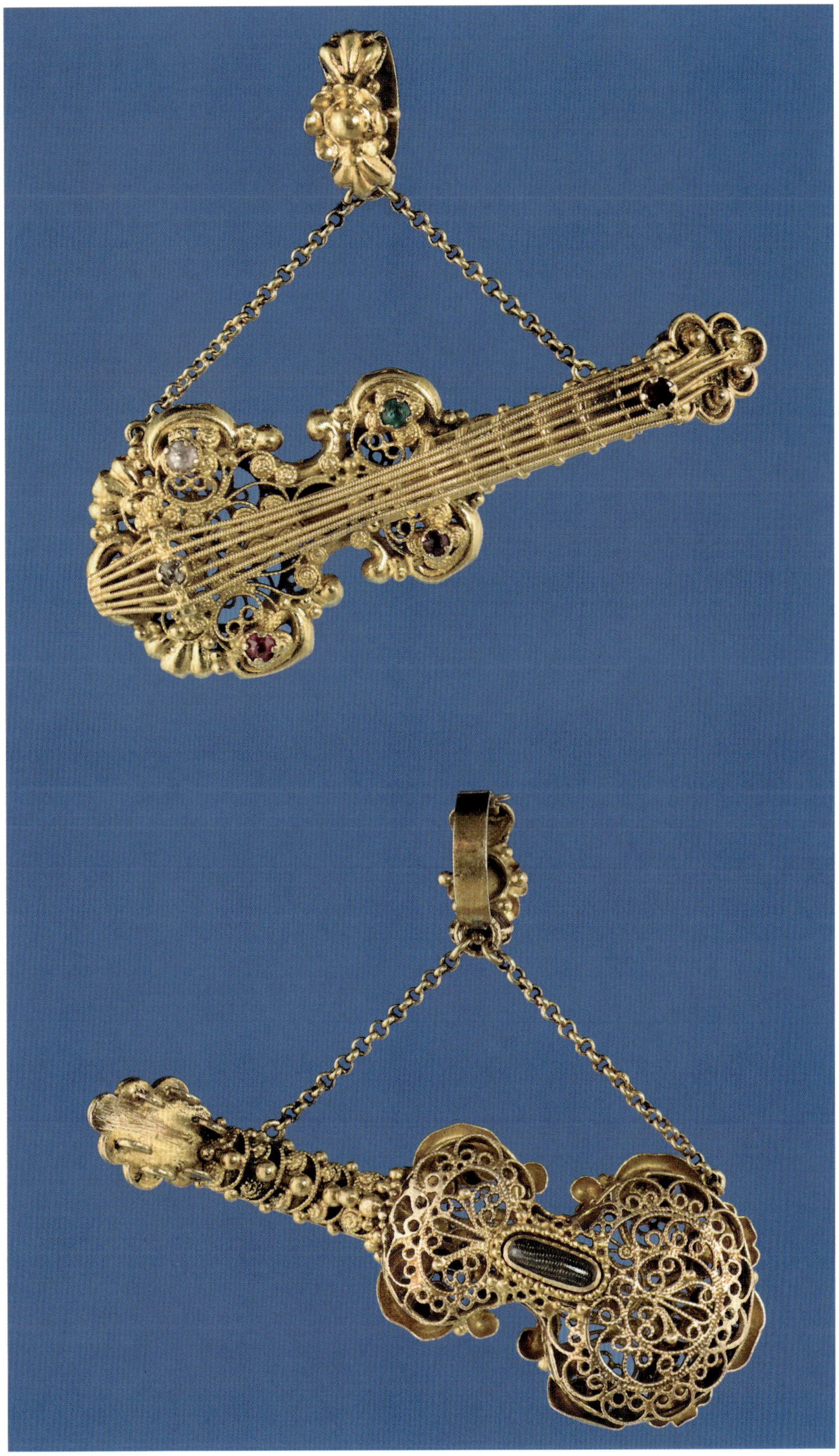

Gold filigree and cannetille acrostic guitar pendant spelling out in gemstones the word 'dear' c.1820, front and back

Flat garnet heart brooch surmounted by crown of love birds c.1750

Animal motifs were also used in love jewellery, such as doves for purity, bees for industry, snakes for eternity and butterflies for the soul. A love bird with an envelope stood for a declaration of love. Moths fluttering around a diamond-topped candle were a warning of the dangers of passionate love. Salamanders (said to thrive in fire) symbolised passion in love and ducks, who were thought to mate for life, stood for marital fidelity.

Above left:
Forget-me-not gold cannetille padlock with gems spelling out 'regard' c.1820

Above right:
Acrostic gold cannetille work double-sided locket spelling out 'regard' on one side and 'dearest' on the other c.1820

Large two-stone specimen ring c.1800

The language of stones

Diamonds and coloured gemstones had special meanings and could be chosen for the intimate acknowledgement of love between couples: diamonds for constancy, sapphires for the soul, emeralds for faith, and rubies for passion. When one sees a two-stone ring set with a diamond and a ruby, it can be interpreted as a pledge of enduring passion between lovers.

Charming love tokens, some in the shape of padlocks dangling tiny keys or hearts, were among the most cherished mementos of the Georgian era, especially if they conveyed a secret message. The first letters of the words for particular gemstones would spell out, in succession, a romantic word or phrase. These acrostic pieces were charming and singled out the wearer as one who was loved openly and dearly. The most often seen of these phrases are:

R uby
E merald
G arnet
A methyst
R uby
D iamond

D iamond
E merald
A methyst
R uby
E merald
S apphire
T opaz

A methyst
D iamond
O pal
R uby
E merald

L apis
Opal
V ermeil
E merald

Moonstone
E merald

F ire opal
Opal
Ruby
E merald
Vermeil
E merald
Ruby

Acrostic jewellery became a fad that spread throughout Europe. A suite of three gold and gemstone acrostic bracelets commemorating the lives of Napoleon and Marie Louise was one of the only jewels ever commissioned by the Empress.

Collection of foiled gemstone pansy (from the French phrase 'pensée à moi' meaning think of me) brooches and butterfly (symbolising the soul) brooch, Portugal and England 18th and 19th century

The language of flowers

Flowers, too, were used symbolically. The rose is the universal symbol of love, the narcissus, self-love. Pansies are for remembrance and came from the French word 'pensée' (meaning think of the giver). Mistletoe was for kisses (and fertility), daisies for purity and innocence, bouquets of flowers stood for the virtues of married life. Sometimes the languages of flowers and stones were combined for double symbolism, as in the case of turquoises, which stood for forget-me-nots, which stood for remembrance. Often we see the motif of the rose with a thorn: 'Jamais la rose sans l'épine' (never a rose without a thorn), meaning love is always accompanied by the danger of being hurt.

Emerald and diamond giardinetti ring and ruby and diamond crowned heart ring c.1780

Portuguese multicoloured topaz daisy brooch c.1780

Foiled pink topaz and gold pansy necklace and aquamarine and pink topaz pansy pendant

18th century floral gemstone brooches

Giardinetti (little garden) rings and brooches were designed as vases or flower-pots of tiny gemstone flowers and were all the rage in Western Europe from 1740 to 1780. They were new in shape to the eighteenth century, with openwork designs in a rococo style. The use of small stones (mounted in gold if they were coloured and silver if they were diamonds) arranged in gay floral settings must have been a breath of fresh air to the world of fashion. These were charming love tokens that were exchanged between couples or friends and

Three giardinetti rings: left to right c.1820, 1770, 1750

Coloured diamond giardinetti ring, Italian 1770

18th century enamel on gold vinaigrette with two-sided inscription 'Ceci n'est rien… L'amitié est tout' meaning 'This is a trifle… friendship is everything' c.1790

Giardinetti brooch photographed on a page from Pouget Fils' book of floral designs published in 1762

whose symbolism was not mysterious, but more like a bouquet of flowers for someone who was much admired.

French amatory jewels enjoyed a vogue in the late 1700s. These were a particularly refined form of love jewellery: navette-shaped pendants and brooches of blue enamel or blue paste in half pearl or enamel surrounds, whose interiors, framed under glass, displayed charming nosegays of seed pearls on a background of hair. Some of them bear inscriptions in French such as 'amour' or 'amitié' or 'A Vous Dédie'. Sometimes these love tokens would display the letter 'M' which stood for 'aimes moi' or love me. Often these jewels were made in England but executed in the French manner.

Opposite:
French amatory jewels of navette-shaped seed pearls on blue enamel fields – lockets and brooches c.1790

Portrait miniature ring painted on ivory with diamond surround 1820

Miniatures

Finely-crafted small portraits, usually on ivory or vellum, were given as love tokens between husbands and wives or parents and children. Miniaturists could capture remarkable likenesses and these could be worn as lockets, rings, bracelets or brooches. The quality of the settings reflected their importance. These could be of plain or chased gold, but the finest have surrounds of diamonds, pearls, or gemstones. Miniatures were also worn as mourning jewellery, or might be tokens of political allegiance or non-romantic friendship.

Miniature of early 19th century American child, Amelia de la Vergne Dodge – all original pendant in foliate cast frame and chain

Miniature of young Englishman, Benjamin Hatley Foote, set in original gilt metal frame and dated 1743 on the reverse

Seed pearl jewellery including necklace with portrait on ivory c.1800

Eye miniatures

A brief fashion was for 'lover's eye' jewellery. An exquisitely painted miniature on ivory of the giver's eye would be presented to the loved one in the form of a brooch, ring or locket, often with a compartment at its back containing a lock of hair. This could then be worn with impunity under the impression that no one would recognise the giver.

On 6 December 1785, Lady Eleanor Butler noted in her diary that a friend who was just back from the Grand Tour showed her 'an Eye, done at Paris and Set in a ring. A true French idea and a delightful idea which I admire more than I confess for its singular Beauty and Originality'. But the ever up-to-date Prince of Wales had already sent a miniature of his eye to his mistress, Mrs. Fitzherbert, with a letter proposing marriage, dated 3 November 1785. The painting was probably done by Richard Cosway or George Engleheart, who were among the leading miniaturists of the time. This particular lover's eye may have been more about fashion than delicious secrecy, for wouldn't the Prince of Wales' eye have been recognisable to almost everyone?

Silhouettes

'Black shades', as these were originally called, began being made around the end of the seventeenth century. Monsieur Etienne de Silhouette, who gave his name to the genre, was merely a gifted enthusiast who covered the walls of his chateau with his efforts, but professionals and amateurs alike delighted in creating minor masterpieces in this now forgotten art. Silhouettes were made by tracing a profile from a shadow cast by a candle on to paper and then reducing it with a machine known as a pantograph. The silhouette was then cut out, painted and framed. The finest practitioners produced quite lovely effects and could charge high prices for their work.

Silhouette by Francis Torand c.1785

Top:
Early 19th century French gold eye miniature ring (with later inscription, 'Christian Febiger bequeathed to J. O'H') and English eye brooch with pearls and blue enamel

Above:
18th century eye miniature in gold locket

Above:
Double sided sentimental gold hair pendant, early 19th century

Opposite:
Large enamelled gold brooch expressing familial love with a 'landscape' of hair on the back, displaying the hair of various family members, Italian or Swiss c.1830

Below:
Lace pins and ring with bezels of hair framed in pearls c.1800

Strands of familial love

While jewellery made using the locks of a loved one's hair, braided into neat little arrangements under glass, has been associated almost entirely with death, this is a modern-day misconception. Much of the jewellery containing hair is, in fact, a token of love and friendship. Women would make up pieces with their children's hair as keepsakes and as heirlooms of the future. Elizabeth Shackleton wrote in her diary in the late 1780s that she had commissioned a bracelet with 'an extreme neat Landscape in my own hair' as well as one made up with the hair of her three (living) sons 'so as to shew all the hair distinctly'. The Duke of Clarence, later William IV of England, wrote to his brother, the Prince of Wales, in 1785 asking for 'a lockit for my shirt with your hair'.

Not always a keepsake of filial, familial, or married love, George IV's passion for hair seems to have been of a different nature. We have this information from diarist, Charles Grenville, who was told by the Duke of Wellington that he had found among the dead King's possessions 'a prodigious amount of hair – women's hair – of all colours and lengths, some locks with powder and pomatum still sticking to them' – souvenirs of the King's long career as a ladies' man.

Gemset French Saint Esprit brooches, late 18th century

Foiled pink topaz crown brooch with cross pendant c.1820

French 'oil and vinegar' foiled quartz cross pendant c.1790

Detail of back of Iberian cross on opposite page

Iberian gold cross with table-set diamonds, second half of 18th century

Love of God (and fashion)

In 1752, the smartly dressed Lady Jane Coke was quoted as saying: 'You can't make a mistake as to the length of your cross. You may either wear it high upon your neck or let the bottom of it touch the top of your stays'.

No other emblem of the eighteenth century was more iconic than the cross. It managed to be, at the same time, both a symbol of faith and a fashion statement. It flashed in diamonds and emeralds upon the décolletés of wealthy Christians in cities all over Europe, but its daily presence glowing at the throats of devout women of the regional provinces was at least as powerful. Shining equally brilliantly in churches, and ballrooms, the emblematic force of the cross as a spiritual symbol and a beautifying adornment has never ceased to mesmerise.

Crosses were of varying designs: the Latin cross, the Greek cross, the Maltese cross and the St. George's cross. Another religious icon is the Saint Esprit. Taking the form of a dove, this is literally the cross of the Holy Ghost and was worn by French peasant women throughout the eighteenth century. Some of these are speckled with dotted enamelling and have foiled crystals with a magical pinkish/red/gold colouring called 'oil and vinegar'.

Filigreed and pierced gold and diamond boxed set, Normandy c.1790

Opposite:
Collection of French provincial gold crosses and Saint Esprit pendants c.1790

Pressed tortoiseshell cameo ring set in gold symbolising a libation to love

Opposite:
Engraving of Hannah Lightfoot after a painting by Sir Joshua Reynolds

Carnal love

Of all the love tokens of the eighteenth century, none is as fascinating as those that celebrate carnal love. Our interest in these special pieces is more curious than prurient because it is hard to imagine overt sexuality in a time of such courtliness and refinement (although the novels and diaries of the time have certainly disabused us of this!).

Below is a unique miniature, painted in America in 1828 by a talented miniaturist named Sarah Goodridge of her own undraped breasts. This was a gift she gave to the famed American statesman, Daniel Webster, with whom she is said to have had a long affair but never married. His descendants called her his fiancée (although he was twice married – to other women) and this miniature along with her easel and paintbox were found among his effects after his death. Coming from a generation that prized female modesty, this miniature is quite shocking. The little beauty mark on her right breast is the most provocative detail of the painting, one that seems to make the point: 'Only you know who I am. Don't forget about me. I am unique'. That Webster never disposed of it seems to prove that she indeed left her mark.

In the eighteenth century a young man's education was finished when his family sent him on the Grand Tour of Europe. Italy was always an essential part of this Tour and many young men became enamoured of antiquities, particularly intaglios from ancient Rome. Many of these were brought back to England and set as rings in oval gold 'Roman' settings. The example shown here is a Nicolo agate of a scarce and unusual shade of blue. The intaglio is first century Roman and was mounted c.1780. Especially curious is the combination of a carved phallus with a butterfly and a snail. Butterflies represent the soul which wings its way from the body at death. The snail represents the evolution of man to spirit. What either of these have to do with the phallus is not known absolutely, but one interpretation might be the hope of the intaglio's carver that sexual fulfilment, a most pleasurable aspect of this life, would continue into the next.

Unusual Roman intaglio in 1780s gold English setting

Extraordinary miniature belonging to American statesman Daniel Webster
The Metropolitan Museum of Art, Gift of Gloria Manney, 2006 (2006.235.74), Photograph © 2006 The Metropolitan Museum of Art

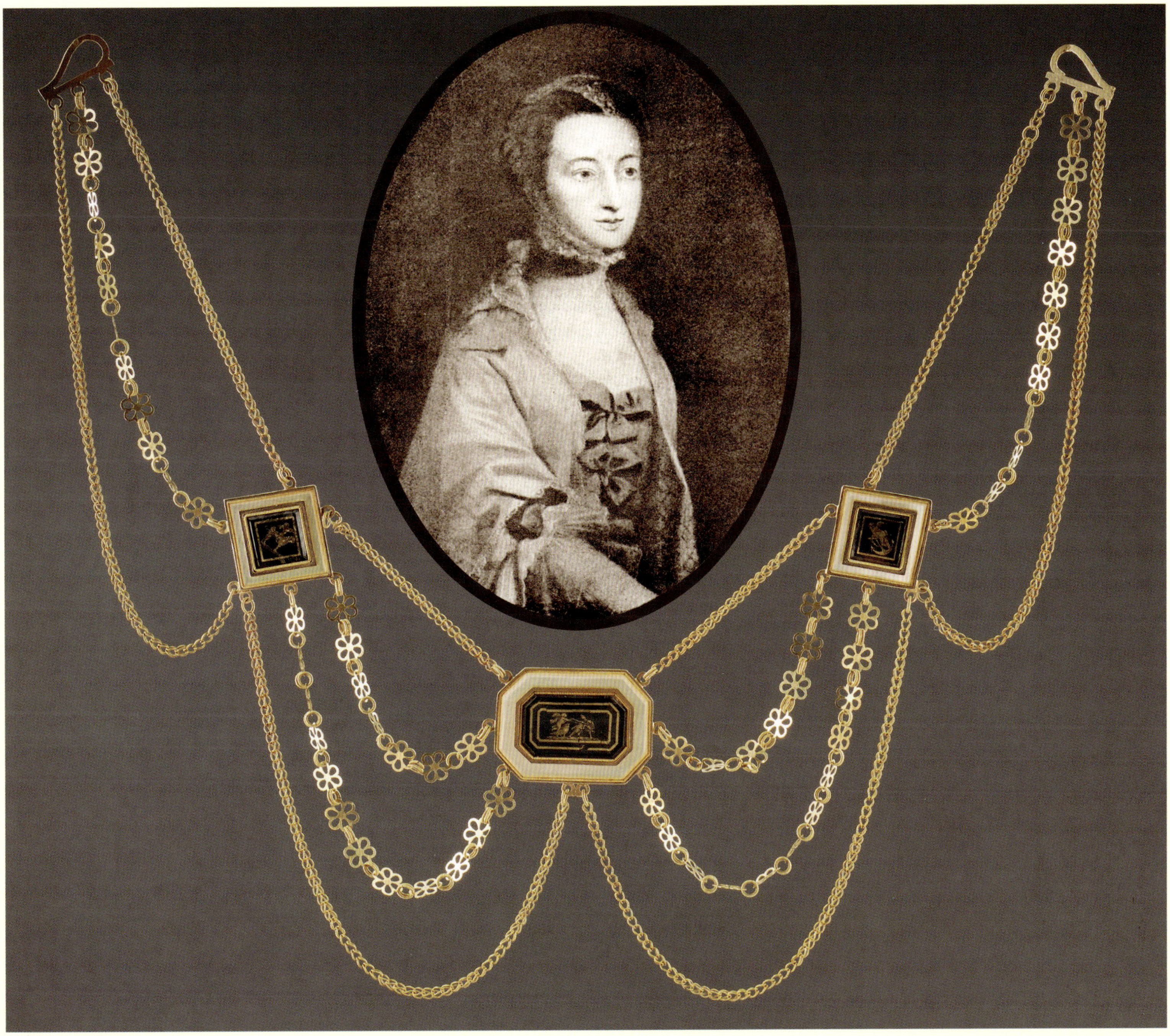

Hannah and the King

There has been much debate about the story of George III's relationship with a Quaker girl named Hannah Lightfoot.

As a young prince, George is said to have seen Hannah while on his way to the theatre one evening and asked one of his ladies-in-waiting to arrange a meeting. Thus began a relationship that flourished for many years culminating in a clandestine marriage, which produced three possible heirs to the British throne.

The royal family disapproved of this love affair and insisted that Hannah marry a grocer named Isaac Axford in a marriage chapel. Mysteriously, she was secreted away immediately after the ceremony and never consummated the marriage and in fact was never seen again. George went on to marry Princess Charlotte Mecklenburg-Strelitz in 1761 amidst rumours of his previous marriage and children.

The oldest of these children, named George Rex, was later given a royal warrant and sailed to South Africa in 1797. He remained there until his death in 1839. He never made a claim to the throne, nor did he marry the mother of his own children, honouring what many historians have believed was a promise to George III never to produce any legitimate heirs that would undermine the British monarchy. The necklace pictured here has been historically documented as having been given by George III to Hannah Lightfoot when he was Prince of Wales and has been passed down for generations in the family of George Rex.

A column of gold and black enamel mourning rings displaying ivory skulls set under crystals, mid-18th century

Chapter 5

Death

Stuart crystal rings, slide, pendant and earrings, early 18th century

Three hundred years ago, death was a way of life. Without the miracles of modern medicine, life expectancy was about half of what it is today. When we examine the memorial jewellery of the eighteenth century, we are often shocked to see inscriptions that indicate how many died young – perhaps of the plague, perhaps of the common cold. Many women and children died in childbirth. Mourning jewellery was a way for the bereaved to hold on to the memory of the loved one who had passed away too soon. In realising the comfort and consolation this must have brought, the customs of Georgian England do not appear morbid or ghoulish, but touching and loving: an appropriate way to honour the dead.

The custom of wearing jewels to commemorate a death began hundreds of years earlier but experienced a great revival in the eighteenth century, possibly as a result of the publication in 1742 of a very popular book called *Night Thoughts on Life, Death and Immortality* by Edward Young. Shortly thereafter, enormous amounts of memorial jewellery began being worn in England and this trend spread to the rest of Europe and America.

Stuart crystals

The execution of King Charles I in 1649 spawned a jewellery industry which produced carved rock crystal stones that were mounted over ciphers made of gold wire, displayed upon a background of hair work, and set in simple gold rings to show support for the monarchy. Some of these are embellished with crowns of gold wire as well. Called Stuart crystals, many of them pre-date the 1700s, but it was from these roots that the popularity of the eighteenth century memorial ring began to grow. Stuart crystals were also made as clasps, cufflinks,

Five rotated views of an exceptional skeleton ring inscribed 'G. Sitwell Arm [army] OB 20 Feb 1722 Aet 66'

earrings, slides and pendants, some with a background of black silk fabric or rose or blue foils added to the hair work. Many of these pieces date from the seventeenth century.

Stuart rings had crystals that were cut flat on top and faceted on the sides, set in bezels that were round, oval, square or diamond shaped. The shanks are usually plain uninscribed gold hoops or have traces of black or white enamel around the bezel.

Mourning rings

By the 1740s the Stuart crystal ring had evolved into the quintessential Georgian mourning ring: a smaller crystal or gemstone-set bezel with a reeded back and the name and dates of the deceased engraved on an enamel and gold scrolled shank. Often, instead of ciphers, these contained skulls or skeletons made of ivory or paper. The more important of these have diamonds set in the ring's shoulders and some have engraved and enamelled skeletons stretching around the exterior of the band with the birth and death dates of the deceased on the underside.

Memorial ring marking the passing of the Reverend Philip Gardner DD Obt 10 Sept 1826 aet 95

Enamel and gold mourning rings dating from 1751 to 1824

Memorial rings were sad and beautiful tokens used to commemorate the death of a family member or loved one. They outnumbered all other types of mourning jewels and were given by all who could afford them. The custom of leaving a provision in one's will for the making and distribution of mourning rings for esteemed friends and family took hold in the latter part of the seventeenth century. Samuel Pepys left 123 rings on his death in 1703. Robert Walpole, Earl of Orford, died in 1745 and left seventy-two rings at a cost of £1 each.

The most often seen examples are the simple gold enamelled bands bearing the name of the deceased and his/her date of birth and departure and sometimes a loving and spiritual inscription on the inside such as 'Gone before but not lost' or 'Sacred to Memory'. While most of these rings are decorated in black enamel, white enamel was used to signify a child or an unmarried person.

By the late eighteenth century, mourning miniatures had become fashionable. These were gentle scenes of sorrow with classically draped ladies swooning against burial urns, worked in hair and mounted on ivory. Navette, oval or

Sepia and hair navette mourning ring commemorating the passing of two teenaged family members within one day of each other. The plinth bears the inscription: 'Sacred to Memory'. The reverse is inscribed: 'Harriett Brown, died 3 July, 1787 ag^{d} 17yrs. Douglas Brown died 2 July, 1787 ag^{d} 19yrs'

Exceptionally fine polychrome mourning brooch with garlands and love birds

Primitive 18th century mourning clasp

Polychrome 18th century mourning pendant of shipwreck

octagon-shaped rings (and also clasps, pendants and brooches), some of considerable size, were executed in monochromatic sepia tones and are moving testaments to the grief of the bereaved. The name of the deceased and the date of death are usually inscribed on the back of the bezel, which is often surrounded by pearls for tears. Sometimes there are pathetic inscriptions on the plinth, such as 'Angels weep when children mourn' and the imagery can be just as heart-breaking: inconsolable maidens, falling trees, broken columns, obelisks and weeping willows. While some of these designs were stock and could be chosen from hair workers' catalogues, some were custom-made and relate to a particular tragedy, such as the one that shows a memorial urn in the foreground and a sinking ship on the ocean behind it – signifying death by drowning. The saddest of all these are the pieces that commemorate the deaths of two or more children in the same family. Sometimes these rings have been shaped as double coffins in crystal, or depict the parents weeping at their tomb, or the inscription on the back shows multiple names with dates of deaths only days apart.

Right: *Extraordinary French mourning brooch depicting four wraiths escaping a gravestone, early 19th century*

Far right: *Mourning pendant depicting the death of two loved ones – the dog is the symbol of fidelity*

Superior blue enamel and diamond mourning ring, late 18th century

Paradoxically, there are memorial rings that seem to defy the very nature of mourning, as in the case of the ring with the diamond bezel pictured on the opposite page showing a woman casually leaning against the plinth with a wine glass in her hand. She seems to be making a toast. Is it 'Good riddance!'? Or, even worse, is that a laugh escaping her open mouth?

From 1795 to 1830 mourning rings again returned to simplicity with an enamelled shank, very often in black and white enamel, with the name of the deceased, age and the date of death inscribed around the bezel encircling an oval, glassed-in locket compartment containing a memento of braided hair. This style of ring is often referred to as a 'cigar band', the shape it most resembles.

From 1810 to 1815 there was a brief trend for mourning jewellery decorated with black enamel snakes with crosshatched golden 'skins'. Signifying eternity, these could be frequently found coiling around the bezels and shanks of rings and the borders of hair locket brooches.

Some mourning jewels are much grander affairs: large blue enamel marquise rings edged with diamonds and featuring diamond urns. These commemorated the more prestigious deaths of those who were, no doubt, just as sincerely missed.

Especially rare and moving are the memorial pieces that contain touching scenes carved out of ivory against a transparent blue or red enamel background and set under glass with surrounds of diamonds which, like the more usually seen pearls, signified the tears of the mourner.

Carved ivory silhouette pendant set against blue glass field with diamond surround, Germany c.1820

Mourning ring depicting lady with wine glass, 18th century

Selection of crosshatched enamel mourning jewels c.1810-1815

Memento Mori

Not all jewellery that used death symbolism was memorial in nature. In the seventeenth and eighteenth centuries there was a fashion for Memento Mori or 'vanitas' pieces, which meant, literally, 'remember you must die'. These pieces were made as humbling reminders of mortality and often used the imagery of skulls, coffins, skeletons and death's heads along with philosophical mottoes such as 'Live to die' to warn the wearer that death awaits us all and that vanity must come to naught.

Mourning pendant exhibiting Memento Mori philosophy, 'The time is unknown but death is certain', 1797

The transition in eye miniatures

By the early nineteenth century 'lover's eye' jewels had a new name, 'tear jewellery', and a new purpose, as sentimental keepsakes of a dearly departed's most soulful feature. Some of these have a tear glistening at the corner of the eye to intimate sorrow and many show the eye peeking through a veil of clouds, perhaps to infer that the loved one might be watching from on high the goings-on of this mortal world.

Below left:
An example of a mourning 'eye' ring c.1820

Below right:
Eye brooch set in gold with diamond 'tear' c.1800

Brooch and necklace fashioned from a loved one's hair c.1820

Hair work in mourning jewels

'Whose hair I wear, I loved most dear' is an old epigram that explains, as much as anything can, the fashion of wearing mourning jewellery containing a loved one's lock of hair. Most mourning rings have little locket compartments for such and forward-looking persons would snip locks of hair to keep ready against the event!

The popularity of hair jewellery was to hold England in its thrall for all of the eighteenth century and the nineteenth as well (perhaps as an empathetic reaction to the death of Queen Victoria's Prince Albert). But hair work was also admired in France and the United States. France became a major producer of sentimental hair jewellery until the Revolution. An advertisement for an American hair working firm effervesces about its products in terms that would make a Madison Avenue copywriter feel right at home: 'Hair is at once the most delicate and lasting of our materials and survives us, like love. It is so light, so gentle, so escaping from the idea of death, that, with a lock of hair belonging to a child or friend, we may almost look up to heaven… and say "I have a piece of thee here, not unworthy of thy being now"'.

Over time it has become increasingly difficult to find untouched mourning jewellery because the hair behind the glassed-in bezel of a brooch, pendant or ring has often been removed and an agate, paste or gemstone has been reset in its place to avoid 'creepy' associations. This has made a mourning ring or brooch saleable to those who would otherwise disdain it, but it has reduced the supply of untouched Georgian memorial pieces.

Carved jet beads, early 19th century

Jet

Jet is a coal-like, carbonised black fossil formed by heat, pressure and a chemical reaction on ancient deposits of driftwood from the *Araucaria*, or monkey-puzzle, tree. It was used during the Bronze Age for small personal articles and again during the Roman era. In medieval England monks in monasteries used jet to fashion rosary beads and crosses, but it really came into its own when a little town called Whitby on the craggy Yorkshire coast began mining the jet from its cliffs, and collecting it from its shores, at the end of the eighteenth century. By 1830 it had begun turning out mourning jewellery for all of England and Europe.

Although jet in Georgian jewellery is most frequently seen today as the small faceted stones that surround the bezels of mourning rings, *The Gallery of Fashion* for the month of April in 1795 reported: 'Jet ornaments, necklaces and earrings' are recommended and again in May 1798 for mourning dress: 'black jet beads and cross'. Women were advised to wear complete parures of jet beads, including extremely long jet earrings and crescent brooches. A jet parure was amongst the lesser suites of jewellery left by the Empress Josephine, divorced wife of Napoleon, who died at the age of fifty in 1814. It was valued at a similar price to a parure of coral. In 1797 Garrards sold mourning

Early carved jet earrings

jewellery described as a 'black bead necklace' and matching earrings, which were probably jet. In the late eighteenth century jet was being worked by hand into faceted beads and crosses until John Carter set up the first jet workshop in Haggersgate, Whitby, in 1808.

Jet jewellery is most often associated with the Victorian era as that is when its use was at its peak. It's no wonder that in Bram Stoker's 1897 novel, *Count Dracula,* the fiendish Count, fleeing the wreck of the schooner *Demeter*, changed himself into a wolf and landed in Whitby, Yorkshire. The crumbling ruins of Whitby Abbey must have appeared eerie and haunted even then, and it seems fitting that the source of the black jewellery which darkened so many throats should be his landing place.

Although, on a cheerier note:

Still, fashions change; maybe some day,
Again the craft will thrive,
And Yorkshire jet will ring the earth,
Black, flashing and alive.

Poem inscribed on the wall of the Jet Miners Arms pub in Whitby

Bog Oak

Another black material used for mourning jewellery in the early nineteenth century was bog oak, fossilised wood which could be found while digging for peat in the bogs of Ireland. While the later bog oak pieces, so favoured in Victorian England, have themes of clichéd carved shamrocks and castles, the Georgian pieces exhibit simple striated or pineapple carving on the beads of its necklaces and bracelets.

Striated bog oak beads, early 19th century

Miniature with heart-shaped diamond surround and crowned urn portraying Georgiana, Duchess of Devonshire, c.1800

Red and white enamel memorial pendant set in gold with hair and pearls under glass, displaying a coronet with four pearls which signify that the commemorated one was a baron or baroness

Pair of Berlin iron snake bracelets Germany c.1820

Mourning Rituals

Traditions in mourning followed a prescribed pattern. Upon the death of a family member or loved one, Georgians were expected to go into full mourning and to wear only black. Activities were severely limited. After a suitable period of time, the bereaved would enter half-mourning when sombre colours such as lavender and grey were introduced again. Finally, after the appropriate passage of time, normal social life, with all its colours, was resumed.

The mourning of royal personages, with its stricter adherences to mourning regulations, always caused an increased demand for memorial jewellery and the symbols of royal bereavement, the snake, the cross, the torch and the crown, were worn around the necks and wrists and fingers of loyal subjects everywhere. Given the high mortality rates of the time, some unfortunate people must have spent most of their lives in black.

Opposite:
The Funeral Ceremony of Her Royal Highness the Princess Charlotte of Wales by Thomas Sutherland NATIONAL PORTRAIT GALLERY, LONDON

England Mourns a Princess

When Princess Charlotte, the only child of the Prince Regent (later George IV) and Caroline of Brunswick, died of complications during childbirth at the age of twenty-one in 1817, Henry Ellis, an accomplished jeweller from Exeter, wrote in his journal: 'Being considered a promising scion of Royalty, brighter days were looked forward to when she should become the occupant of the throne instead of her profligate and licentious father… articles of mourning were in such demand that all the stock of black in the Kingdom came into request'. Charlotte's death was mourned nationwide. American ambassador, Richard Rush, reported that when he arrived in England in 1817, at Christmas time, the entire populace was plunged in grief and dressed in black and he was struck by the atmosphere of national bereavement.

The untimely death of Princess Charlotte precipitated a crisis for an heir to the throne. The Prince was estranged from Queen Caroline (but still legally married) and was certainly not contemplating further children with her. His second brother was married but childless, so the three younger brothers were instructed to marry and have offspring immediately. They all chose German princesses and the new Duchess of Kent, formerly Victoria, Princess of Leiningen, duly gave birth to a healthy baby girl, Alexandrina Victoria, who became Queen Victoria in 1837. During her reign, Queen Victoria, suffering the loss of her beloved Prince Albert in 1861, would take England's mourning conventions to blacker depths than ever before.

A rose cut diamond snake ring and rose cut diamond earrings, late 18th century

Chapter 6

Eternity

Exceptional knitted gold tubular chain with ball clasp c.1810

Collecting Georgian Jewellery

Should you desire to own and/or collect Georgian jewellery, it's advisable that you approach the marketplace well focused and well schooled, not to mention well heeled! These days you can still find eighteenth century jewellery in many places: fine department stores, well-known antiques markets, cyclical antiques shows and exclusive jewellery shops (see page 189 for a list of some of the best). Although the quality and rarity of pieces will vary from opportunity to opportunity, it is still possible to find an amazing gem for a reasonable price, if you are sharp of eye and persistent. For a true collector, the fabulous find is the ultimate serendipity.

Here are a few guidelines for successful and safe buying: Try to learn a bit about what you're buying before you begin. Since so many precious pieces were remodelled during their long lives, one of the best ways to learn about Georgian jewellery is through the study of the still existing parures made of less precious stones that meticulously copied them. In fact, inexpensive jewellery often tended to be more *au courant* and fashionable and that's why some of the most interesting and quirky pieces to be found today are made of secondary materials.

Always buy from dealers you know to be reputable. Never buy anything without a receipt that describes what the item is, what it is made of and when it was made. If you are purchasing a piece as an investment, ideally it should be in perfect condition. But, if you are buying it to wear, or just because you love it, you may decide to take it 'as is'. Many dealers do not want to be bothered repairing every little indication of wear and have priced their less than perfect pieces accordingly. One rule of thumb is that, if you feel you are getting a real bargain, be sure to look the piece over carefully. It may not be as much of a bargain as you think. It's a good idea to carry a jeweller's loupe. It's amazing how much more one can find out about a piece when seen under magnification.

Facts and Findings

Out in the antiques marketplace, try to become familiar with the findings and fittings on Georgian jewellery. Be sure to notice the backs of earrings, the pin-backs of brooches, the types of clasps, the varieties of Georgian chain, and other special idiosyncrasies that are the signposts of authenticity. Learn to recognise quality and, in general, avoid pieces that are suspiciously new looking. Look for pieces with inscriptions – they are a valuable part of a piece's history providing the date of its original ownership and its purpose. In earrings, look for ones that are mirror images of each other and have, design permitting, a left and a right side, rather than each of the pair being identical. In bracelets, look for those that have retained their original clasps and look for pairs: like complete suites of jewellery, they are always more valuable than singles. In necklaces, also, look for original clasps, and always take notice of the graduation of the segments. Georgian jewellers would have made each segment slightly bigger than the one preceding, whereas reproductions would have only a few differing sizes of graduation or would be uniform, as this would be a much cheaper way of making them.

Back of garnet and topaz stomacher set in silver, see page 179

Adaptations

As antique jewellery continues to disappear into private collections all over the world, opportunities to buy authentic pieces are getting scarcer. There are many antiques in not-original condition that have been creatively repaired, joined or converted at a later time. The attitude towards these pieces has been changing recently. First of all, very few truly old pieces have managed to come through two hundred years without some repairs – in fact, it shows they were loved and valued. Pieces that have been 'married' are sometimes brilliant inspirations and sometimes not. If you are considering one of these, look it over carefully, and if the conjoined parts have been wedded to form a blissful whole, it's probably not a problem. Once frowned upon by purists, newly-converted pieces – such as buttons changed into rings, aigrettes into brooches and single earrings into pendants – are now quite acceptable. A great deal of antique jewellery has had a history of renovations, as fashions were always changing, and many pieces were actually designed to convert into something else, such as tiaras into necklaces. To take something today that was obsolete and not very wearable and give it new life can be an admirable and worthy effort. One dealer told us that, in the past, she would never even look at a Georgian diamond 'button' ring (a ring made from a large diamond button off a gentleman's frock coat), much less buy it; now she says that she'd buy as many as she could find, *if* she could find them!

High quality pavé-set old cut diamond button c.1780, converted to ring

---

Opposite:
Above: *Portuguese gemstone hair ornaments, second half of 18th century, converted to brooches more recently*

Below: *Late 18th century English pavé-set buttons converted to brooches*

Lying eyes

Fakes

There are many reproductions on the market. This is the biggest problem dealers and collectors face these days. Sometimes the reproductions are good enough to fool even experts and the jewellery makers who are turning them out are as shameless as they are tireless. Here are some of the obvious, and not-so-obvious, pitfalls to avoid while seeking out those eighteenth century treasures:

1. If you see the telltale signs of modern techniques, tool marks or materials, be wary of the age of the piece.

   Look at the construction of a piece. Original pieces were most often made from silver or gold sheet and fabricated from scratch. In new reproductions usually a mould is taken of, say, a ring from which castings are made. Every scratch and imperfection of the original will be present in a cast piece, including the telltale 'orange skin' finish (where bubbles had appeared in the gold or silver and been polished out). Also, notice the weight of a piece. If it feels heavier than it should, it might be because it was cast from a mould.

   Look at the settings. The modern jeweller would probably not go through the time-consuming effort of making settings airtight. If the stones don't seem to fit the settings exactly, this is a signal that the piece might not be what you want it to be.

   Look at the oxidation on a piece (the natural discoloration of metal). This is sulphide which builds up naturally over time and differs in colour and intensity depending on where the piece has been kept. An oxidised finish can be created instantly by dipping the piece in a sulphuric solution, which will give it a very matt black even finish. When you see this finish it can be a tip-off that the piece is not old, as it has been purported to be, or has had a major repair, which has left it stripped of its natural colour.

2. If there are no signs of wear, or the piece feels sharp to the touch in places where it should have been rubbed smooth over the years, don't jump to the conclusion it was put away two hundred years ago and never worn. Most Georgian jewellery will show some indications of having been used. However, to confuse you further, there are genuine pieces, sometimes referred to as 'deed box jewellery', which were part of an estate and passed from generation to generation as an inheritance but kept for the value and/or the sentiment in a safety deposit box in pristine, unused condition.

3. If you see more than one or two of anything that you have been told is rare – it probably isn't.

4. If a piece shows abnormal characteristics in design or manufacture for its genre, it's easy to want to believe it's an antique one of a kind, but it's much more likely to be the work of a creative modern jeweller.

Creativity is the name of the game when it comes to fakes. A few years ago Georgian rose cut diamond rings became the jewels *du jour*. It was hardly longer than *le jour suivant* before unscrupulous opportunists began turning out

Grave robbers

adorable little rose cut rip-offs. The rose cuts in most Georgian rings are often not big enough or perfect enough to be the reason a ring is desirable – it's all about its charm and age. Consequently, these fakes, which misrepresent the age of the piece, can be made cheaply (with inexpensive stones imported from India and Turkey) and sold for a good deal of money.

Some things are so rare, such as eye miniatures, that to see any at all should put one on alert. Unprincipled individuals are taking Georgian lace brooches and rings (the kind that have central compartments containing braided hair or foiled paste), popping out the bezels and replacing the contents with newly painted 'Georgian' eyes or old ones cut from eighteenth century miniatures on ivory. Remember, this was a brief fad and more of these 'lover's eyes' have made their appearance in the last twenty years than might have in the entire Georgian period! Similar things are happening with 'regard' and 'dearest' rings. Jewellers take old six- or seven-stone rings, remove the pearls, pastes or garnets and fill them with little gemstones that spell out 'sweet nothings' acrostically. Sweet nothings are what you are buying, if you fall for these. 'Skeletonia' is also in the death grip of modern artistes who are now fashioning all manner of 'rare' skulls and skeletons. Many of their macabre creations reside behind the glassed-in bezels of old pieces whose original residents have been relegated to the graveyard because they wouldn't bring nearly as much in the marketplace. Needless to say, none of the above 'marriages' would be considered acceptable adaptations.

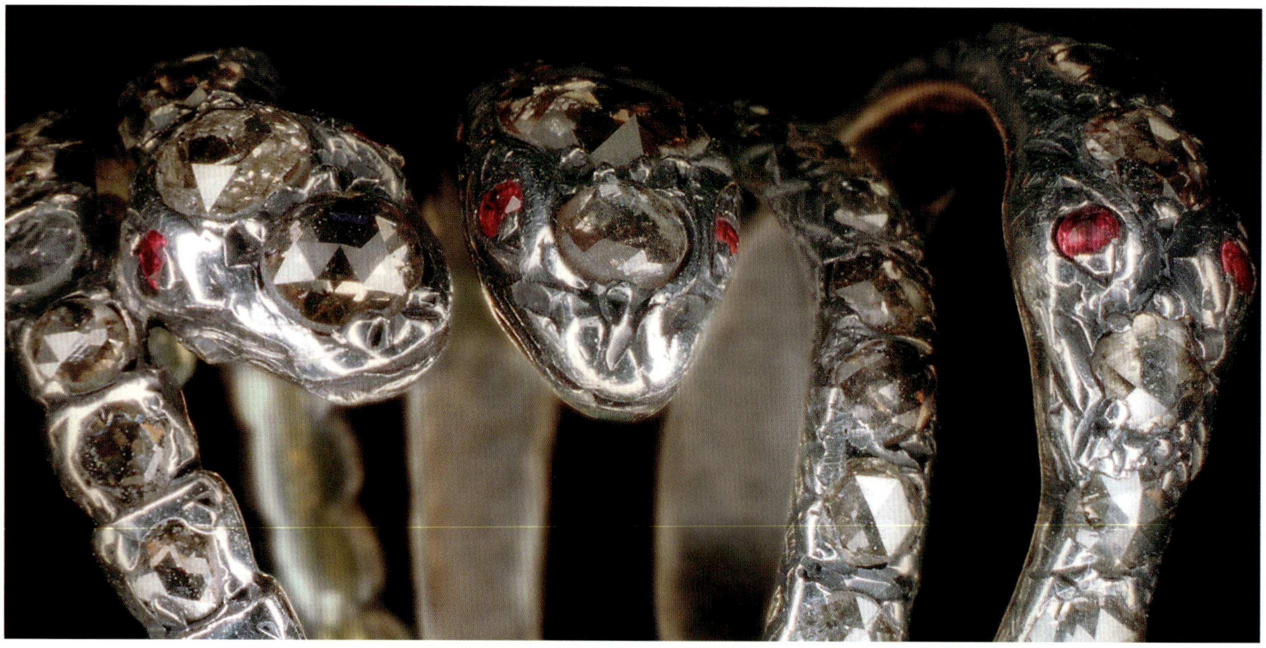

Snake non-charmers

Jewellers are also making brand new 'antique' jewellery as the veritable snake pit of diamond serpent rings that have hit the market will attest. The picture above shows three that were bought in London during one three month period and sold in reputable stores as fully authentic Georgian rings. But notice how all three snakes have the same head, the same eyes, the same expression and the same workmanship, which is crude and shoddy compared with that of an authentic one (see page 170). That three rings made by one particular jeweller two hundred years ago would all have arrived at the marketplace almost simultaneously is just too implausible. It's the same with reproduction giardinetti rings. These delightful 'little gardens' are proliferating faster than weeds and need to be pulled out! A few years ago an entire coffer full of 'Queen Anne' necklaces was unleashed upon an unsuspecting public and, before dealers or collectors could put two and two together, each week another oversized foiled necklace in a garish colour was vied for and snapped up.

Reproduction Georgian chains

Gold Georgian chains are frequently reproduced. Because of the inherent lightness, the gold content is minimal, but the value of a long chain that is genuine is extremely high. This makes it a perfect object to copy. One way of discerning whether a chain is Georgian or repro is to examine the textured links and, if the pattern on the outside is visible on the inside, it points to modern manufacture. Machine stamping techniques are firmer than the original method of rolling the design on the gold and show through the metal. Each curved link should be soldered closed with an almost invisible seal. A complete chain should always be approximately 42in. (105cm) long (to tuck in a lady's waistband), although there are shorter variations. Pinchbeck chains are seldom reproduced as their value is less than those made of gold.

Georgian jewellery is never signed and rarely seen with hallmarks. (Assayers' marks are only found on wedding and mourning bands from the mid-1700s onward.) Georgian jewels were almost always made from gold sheet and wire of 18 carat or 22 carat purity which equated with the coin standard of the time. Some gold French and Russian eighteenth century pieces do bear assay marks.

Auctions

Although auctions can sometimes be a convenient way of disposing of jewellery which isn't authentic, they may just as often offer the careful buyer the opportunity to purchase a genuine piece which may even have a traceable provenance. Auction houses don't take responsibility for the authenticity of a piece, however, so don't necessarily expect recourse if you buy a fake.

Auction buyers need to be aware of how these establishments operate. Auctions are not always very discriminating when they accept items from consignees. They take pieces of all ages and quality levels – anything they feel will bring them the required buyer's and seller's premiums which, combined, now add up to 40% and more. When they prepare their catalogues they have been known to take modern items masquerading as antiques and sometimes include them in photographs of groupings of genuine old pieces. To further confuse the unwary buyer, they estimate some of these pieces as highly as if they were authentic. They omit describing the age of doubtful pieces rather than saying 'modern reproduction of Georgian bracelet' or 'bracelet made in the Georgian style'. Unfortunately for buyers, most auction houses embrace an 'if you don't ask, we don't tell' policy.

If you are thinking of buying an antique jewel at auction, but cannot go to see it for yourself, it is imperative that you ask for a condition report and inquire as to the age of a piece. Then and only then will an auction appraiser tell you what you need to know in order to place your bid with confidence. Even then, it's *caveat emptor* with auction houses.

Online auctions are probably the most risky place to buy antique jewellery. Although there are some nice things sold online by good people who have inherited a bit of jewellery and live too far away from a major city to sell it there, these are the exceptions that prove the rule that one shouldn't buy a piece one can't handle and inspect in person. Remember that there are scouts looking for fabulous antiques everywhere and they would be the obvious conduit for the sale of fine jewellery. Some online sellers consistently put up dubious pieces and manage to command high prices for such things as eye brooches, imaginatively painted on paper (rather than on ivory) with long mascara'd eyelashes and memento mori rings so horrible that they look as if they were forged yesterday at the very gates of hell! If you must buy online, try to buy from only those dealers who have perfect track records and solid return policies. Once again, if it looks too good to be true, especially on your computer screen, it's probably because it is.

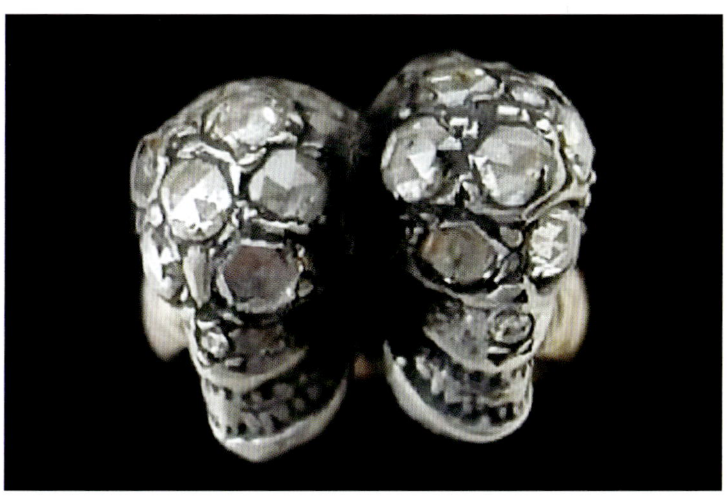

Skullduggery

Three large single stone foiled paste rings set in gold c.1790. Top and bottom are paste, centre is amethyst

Opposite:
Portuguese stomacher with topaz and Hessonite garnets set in silver, c.1715, 4½in. long

Care of Georgian jewellery

The conservation of your Georgian jewellery is of utmost importance. As with anything a few hundred years old, you may need to find a talented repair person, should one of your treasures suffer serious harm. Never try to repair it yourself. Much damage has come to jewellery at the well-meaning hands of those who loved it best!

Never give a Georgian piece to a jeweller for ultrasonic cleaning. The hot ultrasonic liquid will damage or destroy patina and dissolve the colour from the foil backing of stones and the delicate watercolour from miniatures. Cleaning carefully with a dry powder (Borax traditionally) and a soft toothbrush will impart a sparkle to your treasure, but, if in doubt, leave it alone.

Gemstones

The biggest problem in the care of Georgian jewellery is making sure the old foils behind the close-backed settings of most of the pieces set with gemstones, or paste, do not get wet or damaged. Do not wear it in the bath or shower! If a piece does get wet and the stone becomes cloudy, you can take it to a good jeweller and see if he has the ability and know-how to re-foil it. There is usually one very clever (and very busy) repairer in almost every metropolitan centre who specialises in antique jewellery and he will be your best bet. Foils also are compromised by heat so if you have a ring that needs to be sized or a brooch that needs a new pin-back, try to find a jewellery repair man who works with a laser machine. Lasers use a very focused and brief heat and can alter your piece with no damage to the foil, although laser repair people charge more for these jobs than the average repair person.

Georgian rings are very vulnerable to continuous use. Try not to wear a Georgian ring with other rings touching it and feel it regularly for loose stones.

Stone replacement and polishing

If your jewellery has a missing or a cracked stone, you might need the services of a good stonecutter. Whether your problem stone is a gemstone, an agate, a turquoise or a coral, there are qualified and specialised lapidaries who can cut a new one for your repair person to set. If you have lost an antique pearl, half-pearl or diamond, your repair man might have a supply of these on hand; if not, there are dealers who are specialists in replacing things such as these.

Stone polishers can give a tired and dull-looking stone a new lease of life. Some stones are fragile and it is always best to ask the polisher whether he thinks you are taking any risk. It's amazing how many pieces can be saved by either competent repair people or candid ones who tell you the truth when you ask for something that's beyond their power to accomplish.

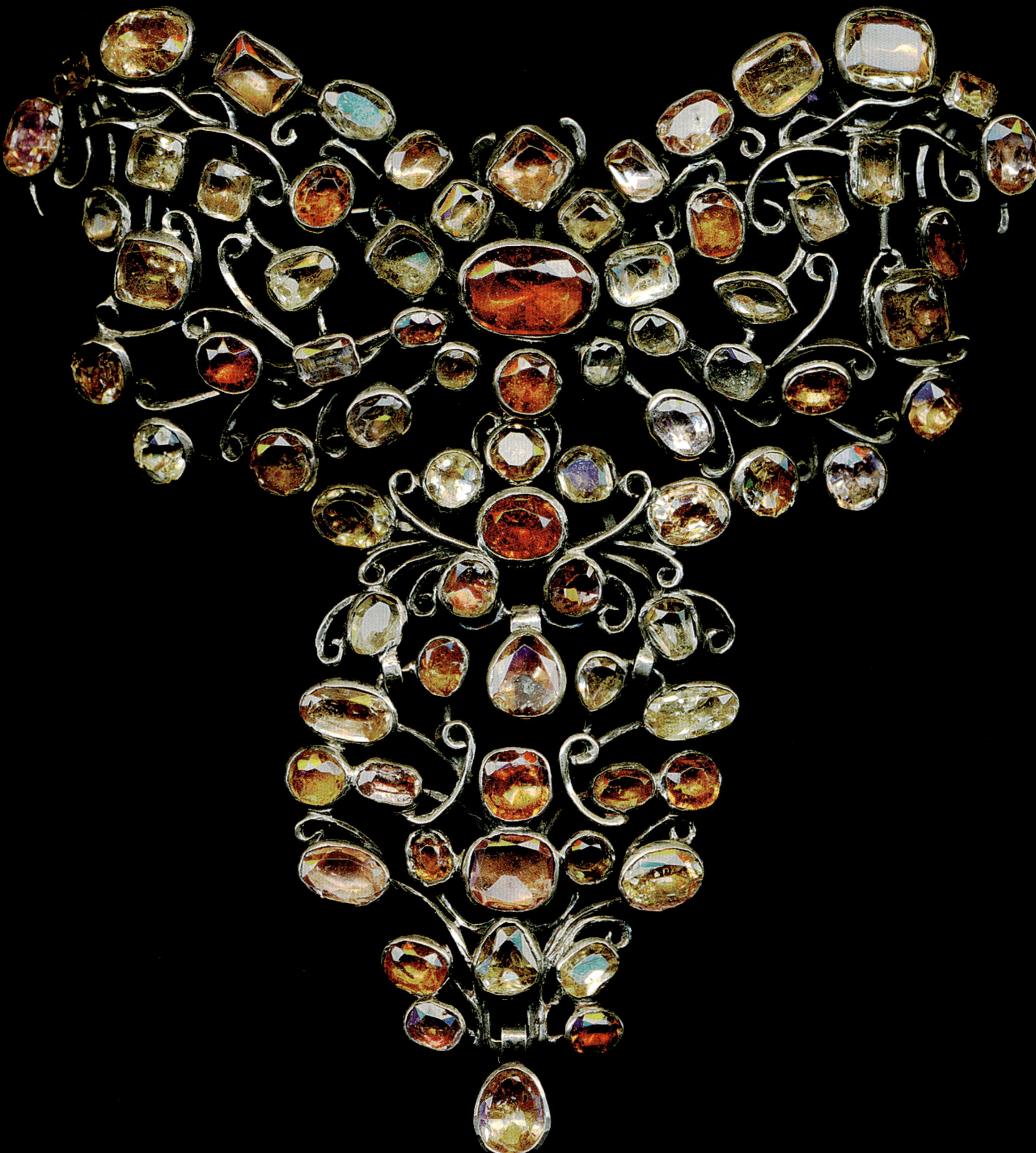

Gold and silver

If the metals of your Georgian jewellery need to be polished, they should not be submerged in any dipping solutions or polished with metal polish. Just gently and carefully run a polishing cloth over the piece. This will remove tarnish if it's silver, or bring up the shine if it's gold.

If the metals need soldering, always ask your repair person to tell you what your risks are. Hard solder is the industry standard but can often jeopardise the patina or foiled stones in a piece. Many jewellers use 'lead' (or soft) solder only as a last resort. Eighteenth and nineteenth century jewellery was often constructed with soft solder (composition 60% tin plus 40% lead). The usual reason was the need for relatively low temperatures to prevent damage to 'soft stones' like coral, pearls, and jet as well as enamel, hair, watercolour and glass. Untidy old repairs that have been done with soft solder can often be improved by a competent repair person. Lead can be removed in some cases but as a simple rule it is often best left alone as the hard soldering afterwards can be very damaging to the old colour and patina. If a piece is in dire need of improvement, the laser is a good alternative to both hard and soft solder.

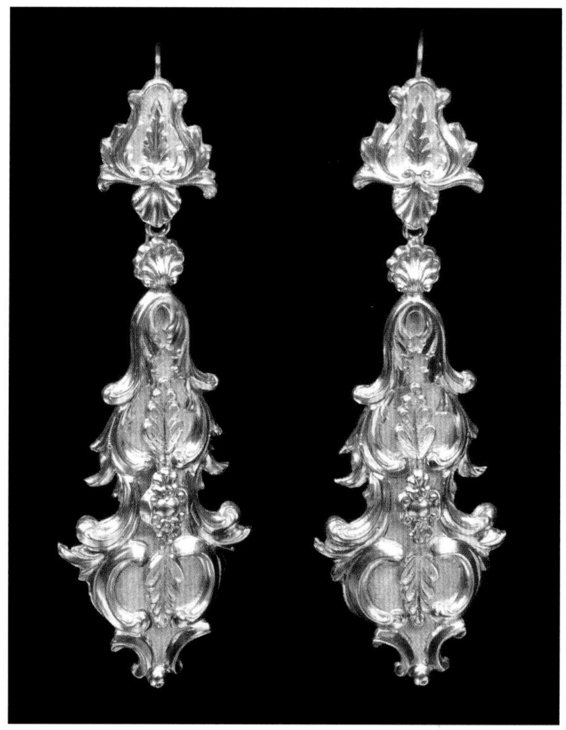

Long rare silver répoussé pendent earrings, first half of 19th century

Steel and iron

Cut-steel and Berlin iron can fall prey to rust if they are exposed to damp or wet conditions. Once rusted, a piece is very hard, if not impossible, to clean. A toothbrush, not too hard, can sometimes remove surface rust from cut-steel. Some books suggest brushing cut-steel with ordinary chromium cleanser, leaving it to dry, then brushing it with a clean brush and polishing it with a soft cloth, but in our experience this has not often helped. Sometimes a dedicated scraping with one's fingernail works better. It has been said that jewellery repair people have a 'trade secret' method of cleaning and polishing cut-steel, so perhaps it is best to leave it to an expert. If you have a rusty piece of Berlin iron, try a light wiping with kerosene or oil. Berlin iron cannot be soldered if it breaks. (Perhaps this will be another job for the laser.)

Investment potential of Georgian jewellery

Kings and queens have held on to their jewels since time began; valuable and talismanic pieces have been hoarded, handed down and treasured by wealthy and aristocratic families; important pieces are documented and reside in museums, private collections and galleries around the world, but most of the treasures in this book were found on the open market during the last few years in London and New York.

Over the last two decades, the prices of fine, antique jewellery have more than doubled. This compares favourably with stock and bond markets and certainly is a better investment than the interest earned on a savings account in your local bank. If you check the evaluations in a reputable antique jewellery price guide such as that by Michael Poynder (ACC Art Books), which has periodic updates, you will see that coral, for instance, in the 1981 Guide quoted at £250, is now standing at an even higher value than when the Guide was last updated in 2000 when it was quoted at £1,000. Today the price would be nearer £2,000. A Berlin ironwork necklace that was £450 in 1981, and £2,750 in 2000, would now probably be more in the region of £4,500.

Spectacular Georgian rose cut diamond foiled earrings c.1800

Perfect parures in original boxes featuring intricate workmanship, natural materials which are fast disappearing and those that exhibit the refined and exquisite techniques of the eighteenth and early nineteenth centuries are the pieces to search out and collect. It's even better if they are also highly wearable. Remember that it is the *best* pieces in the *best* condition that *best* retain their value. Jewellery as an investment may not be uppermost in your mind when you buy a piece, but a fabulous diamond ring or stunning cut-steel necklace might easily be more gratifying than stocks and shares and ought to give you a good return, should you ever decide to part with it. Some modern jewellery can be expensive yet, once purchased, it has little resale potential, whereas good antique jewellery will always be resalable.

As with any area of art and antiques, fashions prevail, so don't buy just for investment, but do buy the best you can afford and only what you love.

What goes around comes around. Gemstone pansy necklace c.1790

Platinum necklace, Délices de Cartier jewelry collection, 2001 PATRICK GRIÉS ©CARTIER

The return of the Comet

Most Georgian jewellery was created as a token of love and esteem and so it remains today. Its celebration of beauty and nature can bring lasting and life-enhancing pleasure to those who appreciate it. Georgian jewellery will never go out of style for long. Like the comet discovered by Sir Edmond Halley blazing across the sky in 1759, Georgian jewellery keeps returning to illuminate the creative force and artistic magnificence of the eighteenth century. No wonder Georgians loved comets and depicted them so often! Georgian jewellery is a virtual comet, streaking across the centuries to illuminate its wearers time after time, again and again.

Bibliography

Agates. London: Natural Museum Publications,1989.

Barlow, Andrew. *The Prince and his Pleasures,* London: British Museum, 1997.

Benjamin, John. *Starting to Collect Antique Jewellery.* Woodbridge: Antique Collectors' Club, 2003.

Bennett, David and Mascetti, Daniela. *Understanding Jewellery.* Woodbridge: Antique Collectors' Club, 1996.

Bernier, Olivier. *The Eighteenth Century Woman.* New York: Doubleday and Co., 1981.

Pleasure and Privilege, New York: Doubleday and Co., 1981.

The World in 1800. New York: John Wiley and Sons, 2000.

Becker, Vivienne. *Antique and Twentieth Century Jewellery.* Colchester: N.A.G. Press,1987.

Fabulous Fakes. London: Grafton Books, 1988.

Berg, Maxine. *Luxury and Pleasure in Eighteenth Century Britain.* Oxford: Oxford University Press, 2005.

Black, J. Anderson. *A History of Jewelry.* New York: Park Lane, 1974.

Burgess, Fred. *Antique Jewelry and Trinkets.* New York: Tudor Publishing.

Bury, Shirley. *Sentimental Jewellery.* London: His Majesty's Stationery Office, 1984.

Rings. Maryland: Stemmer House, 1984.

Jewellery, The International Era, Volume I. Woodbridge: Antique Collectors' Club, 1991.

Campbell, Mark. *Self-Instructor on the Art of Hair Work.* New York and Chicago: M. Campbell, 1867.

Clifford, Anne. *Cut-Steel and Berlin Iron Jewellery.* Bath: Adams and Dart, 1971.

Davenport, Cyril. *Jewellery.* London: 1905.

Dawes, Ginny and Davidov, Corinne. *Victorian Jewelry.* New York: Abbeville Press, 1991.

Donald, Diana. *Followers of Fashion.* London: Hayward Gallery Publishing, 2002.

D'Orey, L. *Five Centuries of Jewellery, National Museum of Ancient Arts, Lisbon.* London: Zwemmer Publishers Ltd., 1995.

Edwards, Ralph, and Ramsay L.G.G. (edited). *Early Georgian.* London: Connoisseur, 1963.

Late Georgian: London: Connoisseur, 1961.

Regency. London: Connoisseur, 1958.

Stuart. London: Connoisseur, 1960.

Egger, Gerhart. *Generations of Jewelry.* Philadelphia: Schiffer, 1984.

Evans, Joan. *A History of Jewellery 1100-1870.* New York: Dover Publications, 1970.

Fales, Martha Gandy. *Jewelry in America.* Woodbridge: Antique Collectors' Club, 1995.

Foreman, Amanda. *Georgiana Duchess of Devonshire.* London: Harper Collins, 1998.

Foskett, Daphne. *Miniatures Dictionary and Guide.* Woodbridge: Antique Collectors' Club, 1987.

Flower, Margaret. *Victorian Jewellery.* London: Cassell and Co., 1951.

Frank, Robin. *Love and Loss.* New Haven and London: Yale University Press, 2000.

Goldemberg, Rose Leiman. *Antique Jewelry: A Practical and Passionate Guide.* New York: Crown Publishers, 1976.

Harmon, Claire. *Fanny Burney.* New York: Alfred A Knopf, 2001.

Hibbert, Christopher. *George IV.* London: Longmans, 1972.

James, Duncan. *Old Jewellery.* Princes Risborough: Shire Publications, 1989.

Joannis, Claudette. *Bijoux des Régions de France.* Paris: Flammarion, 1992.

Jones, William. *Precious Stones.* London: Richard Bentley and Sons, 1880.

Joyce, Kristin and Addison, Shellei. *Pearls.* New York: Simon and Schuster, 1993.

Kendall, Hugh. *The Story of Whitby Jet.* Great Britain: Whitby Museum.

Kunz, George Frederick. *Rings for the Finger.* New York: J.B. Lippincott Company, 1917.

Levi, Karen (edited). *The Power of Love.* London: Diamond Information Centre, 1988.

Lewis, M.D.S. *Antique Paste Jewellery.* Boston: Boston Book and Art,1970.

Luthi, Ann Louise. *Sentimental Jewellery.* Princes Risborough: Shire Publications, 1998.

Marquardt, Brigitte. *Schmuck.* W. Germany: Kunst and Antiquitäten, 1983.

Marshall, Rosalind and Dalgleish, George. *The Art of Jewellery in Scotland:* London: HMSO Bookshops, 1991.

Martin, Joanna. *Wives and Daughters: Women and Children in the Georgian Country House.* Cambridge: Cambridge University Press, 2004.

Mascetti and Triossi. *The Necklace.* New York: Harry N. Abrams, 1997.

Earrings. London: Thames and Hudson, 1990.

Mascetti, Daniela. *Oreficeria Del Settecento.* Italy: Insitituto Geografico de Agostini, 1985.

Metelerkamp, Sanni. *George Rex of Knysna.* Capetown: Howard Timmins, 1939.

McSwiggan, Kevin. *Silhouettes.* Princes Risborough: Shire Publications, 1997.

Muller, Helen. *Jet Jewellery and Ornaments.* Princes Risborough: Shire Publications, 1980.

Muller, Priscilla. *Jewels in Spain 1500-1800.* New York: Hispanic Society of America, 1972.

Munn, Geoffrey. *The Triumph of Love.* London: Thames and Hudson, 1993.

Newman, Harold. *An Illustrated Dictionary of Jewellery.* London: Thames and Hudson, 1981.

Oman, Charles. *British Rings 800-1914.* New Jersey: Rowman and Littlefield, 1973.

Percival, MacIver. *Chats on Old Jewellery and Trinkets.* London: T. Fisher Unwin,1912.

Phillips, Clare. *Jewels and Jewelry.* New York: Watson-Gupthill Publications, 2000.

Porter, Roy. *English Society in the 18th Century.* London: Penguin, 1982.

Poynder, Michael. *The Price Guide to Jewellery.* Woodbridge: Antique Collectors' Club, 1976; 2nd revised edition, 2000.

Pouget J.H. *Traité des Pierres Precieuses.* 1762.

Ribeiro, Aileen. *Dress in the Eighteenth Century.* New Haven and London: Yale University Press, 2002.

Rowan, Michele. *Nineteenth Century Cameos.* Woodbridge: Antique Collectors' Club, 2004.

Scarisbrick, Diana. *Jewellery.* London: Batsford, 1984.

Rings. London: Thames and Hudson, 1993.

Jewellery in Britain, 1066-1837. Great Britain: Michael Russell, 1994.

Schiffer, Nancy. *The Power of Jewelry.* Pennsylvania: Schiffer Publishing, 1988.

Speight, Alexanna. *The Lock of Hair.* London, 1871.

Tillander, Herbert. *Diamond Cuts in Historic Jewellery, 1381-1910.* London: Art Book International, 1995.

Vickery, Amanda. *The Gentleman's Daughter.* New Haven and London: Yale University Press, 1998.

Wise, Richard. *Secrets of the Gem Trade.* Massachusetts; Brunswick House Press, 2003.

Catalogues

Tait, Hugh (edited). *The Art of the Jeweller – A Catalogue of the Hull-Grundy Gift to the British Museum.* London: British Museum Publications, 1984.

Dangerous Liaisons. New York: Metropolitan Museum of Art Exhibit 2003.

The Jeweler's Eye. Yonkers: Hudson River Museum, 1986.

William Ernst Moutoux *Illustrated Catalogue of Hair Jewellery.* New York: R.A. Welcke, 1883.

Rings from Antiquity to Present Day. London: Christie's, 1989.

Journals

Thomas Creevey's Papers 1793-1838. England: Penguin, 1948.

The French Journals of Mrs. Thrale and Doctor Johnson. New York: Haskell House Publishers, 1973.

The Diary of Fanny Burney. Ed. Lewis Gibbs. Everyman, Dent, 1971.

Magazines and Periodicals

The Lady's Magazine 1818, *La Belle Assemblée* 1824, *Godey's Lady's Book and Magazine, Harper's Bazaar, Illustrated London News, The Queen, The Jeweller's Weekly, Parisienne Illustrated Review, Young Ladies' Journal, Illustrated Household Magazine, Illustrated Exhibitor and Bon Accord, a Scottish Journal.*

Credits

(in alphabetical order under first name)

Anthea, Grays Antique Market, London, 134 upper left

Barneys New York, 19, 26 bottom, 46, 105 top, 140 lower left, back endpapers: bottom rivière

Brian and Lynn Holmes, London, 36 lower left, 36 lower right (silver chain), 50 bottom

Cartier, 185

Charlotte Sayers, Grays Antique Market, London, 12, 36 lower right (gold chain), 41 upper right, 43 lower right

Corinne Davidov, Washington D.C., 99

Cry for the Moon, John Owen, Guildford, 83 top

D.K. Bressler & Company, Ronald Kawitzky, 32 W. 47 St., New York, 22 top, 55, 135 upper left, 149

Elle Shushan, Philadelphia, 146 upper right (two miniatures), 147 lower right (eye locket)

Famous Antiques, Jim Davies, Bath, 54

Ginny Dawes, New York, 5, 11, 26 top, 32, 40, 41 left and bottom right, 65, 72 right, 76, 82, 85, 89 top, centre right, bottom far left and far right, 90, 91, 101, 110, 135 (except upper left), 141 (except lower right), 142, 155, 156, 170, 181, 184, 186, back endpapers: top four rivières, girandole brooch

Gray and Davis Ltd., Gray Boone, 32 W. 47 St., New York, 56, 61, 62 far left, 86 (earrings and upper ring), 88 bottom, 168 top right

Greens of Cheltenham, Cheltenham, 152, 154 lower left

Hannelore Hetteling, London, 108 upper right

Henry Polissack Antique Jewelry, Northampton, Mass., antique jewellery books

Ian Stanley, The Teacup Arcade, Portobello Road, London, 141 lower right

Jacky Jacoby, Silver Fox Galleries, Portobello Road, London, 42 bottom right and left, 63, 89 (ring) bottom row centre, 111, 124 right

The Jewellery Exchange, Michele Rowan, Grays Antique Market, London, 161 lower right

Julie Seitzman, 74

Kentshire Galleries, New York, 21 top, 60, 73, 78, 89 (ring) centre row left, 120 bottom, 139 upper right

Larkspur and Hawk, Emily Satloff, New York, 13, 33 lower right, 37 top, 43 top, 48 lower right, 51, 58 top, 86 top (lower ring), 107 upper left, 116, 117, 120 centre, 136 top, 137 bottom left, 140 upper right, 143 bottom left (centre ring), 180 (bottom ring)

Leah Gordon Antiques, Manhattan Art and Antique Center, New York, 59 (earrings)

Linda Morgan Antiques, New York, 45 upper right, 93 top, 94 (pavé earrings and clasp), 100 right, 138 right, 146 (miniature pendant necklace) bottom, 147 upper right (eye brooch), 150 lower centre, front endpapers: top necklace

Lowther Antiques, Pat Novissimo, Central Galleries, Portobello Road, London, 10 left, 24, 33 top, 37 bottom, 48 lower left, 119 right, 132, 136 lower left, 139 garnet heart brooch, 143 lower left (ring on right), 146 rings and bracelet bottom photo, 148 bottom, 153, 158, 159, 160 bottom, 161 top centre and right, 164 top, 168 upper and lower left, 175

Madeleine Popper, 64

Melody NYC, Manhattan Art and Antique Center, New York, 59 (necklaces), 86 top (necklace), 94 (harp brooch), 100 left, 109 lower right, 137 top

Michael Longmore, Grays Antique Market, London, 136 bottom centre

Olivia Collings Antiques, London and New York, 2, all but girandole earring, 14 cross, 16 top, 18, 23, 45 bottom, 58 bottom, 62 right, 75 top, 79, 80 top left, 92, 93 bottom, 98, 106 top, 108 bottom, 109 upper left and right, 114 top right and bottom, 119 left, 120 top; 122 upper left, 126 top, 139 left, 143 lower right, 146 upper left, 151, 161 upper left, lower left, 164 lower left, 166, 167, 172, 174, 182, 183

Pam and Doug Brown, Vancouver, 81 bottom

Patricia Taub, 163 top

The Pearl Antiques, Edith Horowitz, Las Vegas, 147 upper right (eye ring)

Peter Hess, Silver Fox Galleries, Portobello Road, London, 144 left, 164 lower right

Pushkin Antiques, Olga, Grays Antique Market, London, 50 top, 113

Ralph Lauren, New York, 102, front endpapers: bottom necklace and earrings

RBR Group, Jo and Olly, Grays Antique Market, London, 36 lower left (gold chain), 81 top, 114 top left, 115 bottom, 138 upper left, 162 bottom

Sian Harlowe, 2 (girandole earring)

Six-Sept, New York, 34

S.J. Phillips Ltd., New Bond Street, London, 10 right, 22 bottom, 28, 30, 53, 70, 72 far left, 75 bottom, 83 lower right, 84, 87, 106 bottom, 107 lower right, 112, 115 top, 121, 122 bottom, 128, 130, 143 top, 144 right, 150 top

The Spare Room Antiques, Baltimore, 140 upper left

Wimpole Antiques, Grays Antique Market, London, 148 top

Index

Page numbers in **bold type** refer to illustrations and captions